Mobsters

Mobsters

A Who's Who of America's Most Notorious Criminals

JOE CORRINA

JG PRESS

Published by World Publications
Group, Inc.
455 Somerset Avenue
North Dighton, MA 02764
www.wrldpub.com

ISBN 1-57215-346-6

Editor: Emily Zelner
Designer: Christopher Berlingo
Production Manager: Ellen Milionis

Printed and bound in China by Leefung-Asco Printers Ltd.

1 2 3 4 5   06 05 03 02

Dedication
For Emily

CONTENTS

Mobsters

A Who's Who of America's Most Notorious Criminals

To say that there was a "golden age" of organized crime may sound ridiculous. By definition, a golden age is a period of great peace, prosperity, and happiness. But all things being relative, peace, prosperity, and happiness depend on perspective. One person's happiness may be another's misery. One person's prosperity may bring another's destitution. Working for peace may in fact seem like waging war, all depending on your perspective.

Organized crime in America reached its maturity during Prohibition, an era that included the decade known as the "Roaring Twenties." This period in American history is marked by great prosperity, a sort of irrational exuberance, to borrow a phrase, despite—or perhaps because of—Prohibition. It certainly was an era of unprecedented prosperity for the bootleggers who delivered illegal alcohol to thirsty Americans. Even when the Roaring 20s came crashing down with the stock market in October of 1929, mobsters still prospered, supplying a way to drown the anguish of the Great Depression.

Even before Prohibition was officially repealed in 1933, mobsters began expanding their enterprises into different areas of crime and vice. More important-

ly, disparate gangs across the country began to organize into a loose collaboration that allowed for an extended period of prosperity and relative peace in the underworld. The national Syndicate provided a structure where previously warring gangs of varying ethnicities, religions, and geographical locations could overlook their differences toward the greater goal of enormous profits from a spectrum of criminal activities, including narcotics trafficking, prostitution, gambling, and labor racketeering.

By and large, this era of relative peace and prosperity in the underworld lasted for several decades after the repeal of Prohibition. This is partly due to the legal and political cover that the mobsters were able to buy. Politicians, police, judges, juries, and witnesses to mob crimes could often be bought, intimidated or eliminated. For decades, the Federal Bureau of Investigations maintained the official view that organized crime simply did not exist in the United States. Such a stance by the premier federal law enforcement agency allowed the national crime Syndicate to flourish and expand, literally helping to chart America's course into the future.

Organized crime obviously still exists in America, although not to the same degree as in years past. In 1962 a reporter for the *New York Herald Tribune* interviewed the mobster Charles "Lucky" Luciano, who at the time was living in Italy, having been deported by the United States government in 1946. The reporter asked Luciano what he would do differently if he had it all to do over again. Lucky replied, "I'd do it legal. I learned too late that you need just as good a brain to make a crooked million as an honest million. These days, you apply for a license to steal from the public. If I had my time again, I'd make sure I got that license first."

This statement could be written off as the cynical views of a career criminal in forced exile. But in light of some of the recent scandals in corporate America, Luciano's assessment isn't so far off the mark. The argument could be made that yesterday's mobsters are today's CEOs. (Although presumably CEOs don't have rivals killed.) But the sheer scale of the willful fraud and disregard for ethics in these cases makes Luciano's remarks particularly incisive and prescient. History is still awaiting the final verdict, but the period when these crooked businessmen were bilking shareholders out of billions was also a time of great opportunity and wealth for many and is generally regarded as a "golden age" of peace, prosperity, and happiness.

But beyond any arguments for a "Golden Age of the Mob," mobsters are also just plain fascinating. It may be that the era of Prohibition was a time of such exuberance because so many people were having fun being bad. People have always had a fascination with the seamy side of life, if not in actual participation, then vicariously through avid reading of murder mysteries, true crime books and novels, tuning in to watch live televised high-speed chases, reveling in real and fictional courtroom drama, or various "reality television" shows to see what people won't do for fame and money. And,

in this same vein, mobsters have achieved a sort of mythological status in America. How many books, plays, musicals, television programs, mini-series, and movies have been devoted to mobsters? How many actors have made careers out of playing these criminals? Rightly or wrongly, mobsters are icons of an era, revered or reviled, but undeniably forever part of American history and culture.

And so here are their stories. Many of these mobsters lived and died decades ago. Over the years, the stories have had a tendency to take on lives of their own. When dealing with the stories of these larger-than-life mobsters, exaggeration, embellishment, and contradiction are par for the course. Much of what is known comes from reporters, biographers, police, or the mobsters themselves, all of whom often have their own agendas. And given that there is no statute of limitations on murder, there is bound to be some hedging of facts along the way. Every attempt has been made to corroborate stories and separate fact from fiction, but the line between the two is not always clear. As a result, there are times when different and often contradictory versions of events are described. The exact truth may never be known.

The list of mobsters in this book is by no means comprehensive, but rather a sort of partial all-star collection that spans roughly six decades. All of the mobsters in this book lived during Prohibition (although a few were just children). Some are famous, others are lesser known. They came from many countries, representing various ethnicities and religions. All are dead. Some died of natural causes, some were murdered, some were executed, and one may have committed suicide. All were criminals. All were mobsters. All were a part of the mob's golden age. Here are their stories.

Prohibition
The Early Years

October 28, 1919:
Volstead Act
passed outlawing
sale and consumption
of alcohol

November 10, 1924:
Dion O'Banion
murdered

January 24, 1925:
Johnny Torrio
shot, retires

January 16, 1920:
Prohibition officially
in effect

May 11, 1920:
Big Jim Colosimo
murdered in Chicago

1919 **1920** **1921** **1922** **1923** **1924** **192**

February 14, 1929:
St. Valentine's Day Massacre

1931:
Joe Masseria *(pictured)*
and Salvatore Maranzano
murdered ending
Castellammarese War

December 18, 1931:
Jack "Legs" Diamond
murdered

November 4, 1928:
Arnold Rothstein
shot, killed

October 17, 1931:
Al Capone
found guilty
of tax evasion

July 1, 1928:
Frankie Yale gunned
down in New York

October 11, 1926:
Hymie Weiss murdered
by Capone forces

926   1927   1928   1929   1930   1931

Prohibition

The Early Years

In 1919, the Volstead Act was ratified as the 18th Amendment to the U.S. Constitution, calling for the outlaw of "intoxicating beverages, and to regulate the manufacture, production, use, and sale of high-proof spirits for other than beverage purposes." For criminals, Prohibition was a license to print money.

Crime was certainly not invented during Prohibition. But what the 18th Amendment did do was to give criminals a relatively easy way to make not-so-small fortunes bootlegging illegal alcohol. With the money they made, bootleggers were able to buy an unprecedented level of legal protection and political influence. Many politicians and cops had always been on the take, but Prohibition raised the ante. Rather than just being able to afford enough to get the cop on the corner to look the other way, wealthy criminals were now able to influence elections, buy politicians, and even choose political appointees.

Another byproduct of Prohibition was the formation of the national crime coalition, known as the Syndicate. The Syndicate sought to organize crime in America, ending the petty feuds and gang wars over race and religion. Standing in the way of its formation, however, were two old school Mafiosi, Giuseppe "Joe the Boss" Masseria and Salvatore Maranzano. The two men fought a battle on the streets of New York at the end of the 1920s and into the early 1930s that came to be known as the Castellammarese War. Named for Maranzano's home town, the small village of Castellammare del Golfo in Sicily, the war was essentially a power struggle fought between Sicilian and non-Sicilian Italians, neither of whom was willing to work with non-Italian mobsters. Ultimately, due in part to their narrowness of mind, neither man won the war.

It was Charles "Lucky" Luciano, Meyer Lansky, and other like-minded mobsters who ended the Castellammarese War, murdering both Masseria and Maranzano in 1931. This cleared the way for the formation of the national crime Syndicate which sought peace and profit for all mobsters alike.

Opposite: Beer is emptied into the gutter as the Prohibition era begins in America.

Left: Kansas had its own Prohibition laws dating from 1880, but they were largely unenforced until Temperance supporter Carry A. Nation began smashing up saloons with her hatchet and bible. She died in 1911, not having lived to see the nationwide "Noble Experiment."

Arnold Rothstein

"If Arnold had lived a little longer, he could've made me pretty elegant; he was the best etiquette teacher a guy could ever have—real smooth."
—LUCKY LUCIANO

I f anyone can be credited with creating organized crime, it is Arnold "The Brain" Rothstein. As mentor to a generation of mobsters, Rothstein was quite literally the model gangster. He was the inspiration for Nathan Detroit in the musical *Guys and Dolls,* and Meyer Wolfsheim in *The Great Gatsby.* Rothstein was what every mobster aspired to be: shrewd, rich, and classy.

Born in 1882 in Manhattan, Rothstein was the second of five children. His father was a merchant who made a fairly decent, honest living. Young Arnold, however, never felt that he belonged. His relationship with his father was strained, with the elder Rothstein constantly praising older brother Harry who was studying to become a rabbi. Uninterested in most subjects except for math, Rothstein left school and home at the age of sixteen to become a traveling salesman. The death of brother Harry only a year later brought Rothstein back to New York. While working as a cigar salesman in order to build up a bankroll, Rothstein honed his skill as a pool player and gambler in the saloons and illegal gambling houses of the city. When he finally saved enough money ($2,000) Rothstein quit his job and became a full-time professional gambler, pool player, and hustler.

Rothstein's skill on the pool table was legendary, beating all comers, often out of large sums of money. He was referred to in the press as "a well-known sports-man." But he had bigger dreams than hustling pool. Rothstein knew that it was money that makes the world go 'round and that in the game of gambling, the only one who always wins is the house. Rothstein decided to become the house.

Upon marrying his wife Carolyn in 1909, Rothstein purchased two brownstones on West 46th Street in Manhattan. One would serve as the family home and the other would house his first carpet joint. The business was a great success with high-stakes gamblers often dropping huge sums. One such payday was courtesy of Percival H. Hill, of the American Tobacco Company, reportedly to the tune of a quarter of a million dollars.

Opposite: Arnold Rothstein poses for a portrait. Rothstein is often credited for having mentored a whole generation of mobsters.

Left: Arnold Rothstein arrives in court in 1928.

Right: Chicago White Sox outfielder Joseph "Shoeless Joe" Jackson was acquitted by a jury of any wrongdoing in fixing the 1919 World Series, but was banned from baseball for life.

Rothstein also had a hand in other businesses both legal and illicit. He began a highly successful bail bonding business, as well as an insurance company. But Rothstein's first love was always gambling. He owned many race horses and won huge sums at the track. Rothstein was so successful that rumors soon followed of impropriety. Whether or not these rumors were true, there is little doubt that Rothstein would take advantage of any information that came his way. One story tells of the time Rothstein discovered that a crooked jockey who was riding for him was intending to throw a race. Rothstein covered all bets against his horse, then switched the jockey at the last minute and

VITAL SIGNS

Born: January 17, 1882
Died: November 6, 1928
Cause of Death: Murdered (shot)
Buried: Union Field Cemetery; Queens, New York

SCREEN TIME

Mobsters (1991). Played by F. Murray Abraham
Eight Men Out (1988). Played by Michael Lerner

cleared three hundred grand in winnings. But the rumors of crooked betting continued to follow him. The most notorious example is the Black Sox incident.

In 1919, eight members of the Chicago White Sox conspired to throw the World Series, which was being played against the Cincinnati Reds. Rothstein was implicated in the plot by several gamblers who had been involved. Apparently Rothstein had been approached to see if he wanted in on the fix. Rothstein contends that he refused the offer, but that his name was probably used to give the plot weight and prestige. Rothstein denied any involvement, telling a grand jury in Chicago, "…I wasn't in on it, wouldn't have gone into it under any circumstances and didn't bet a cent on the Series after I found out what was underway. My idea was that whatever way things turned out, it would be a crooked Series anyhow and that only a sucker would bet on it." The jury believed him, and Rothstein's name was cleared of any wrongdoing. But the scandal would forever be linked with his name.

Another story about Rothstein shows his power among government officials. It tells of a floating card game that was raided by cops. The cops hadn't announced their arrival when they banged on the door and were greeted with a hail of bullets. Several officers were hurt, and an investigation into the incident found Arnold Rothstein as the only armed man at the game. In the ensuing trial, Rothstein was cleared of all charges. Rumor had it the wheels of justice had been greased with $30,000. Dominic Henry, a zealous prosecutor, unwisely pushed for a conviction and ended up on trial himself, facing charges of perjury for which he spent five years behind bars, his career in shambles. The moral of the story? Justice could be bought for the right price, and Rothstein could afford that price.

Prohibition for Rothstein, as with other mobsters, was a goldmine. His foray into rumrunning brought him in contact with many of the up-and-coming mobsters of the day, including Lucky Luciano, Meyer Lansky, Bugsy Siegel, Louis Buchalter, and Frank Costello. Many considered Rothstein to be a mentor. He was a smart, classy, shrewd businessman who could make gentlemen out of street hoods, teaching them not only how to run organized rackets and increase profits, but also how to dress for success and to use proper manners and etiquette. But despite his outward polish and claims of innocence in crooked gambling, Rothstein was a man out to make money, and money wasn't only limited to rolling the dice and rumrunning. Rothstein saw money to be made in narcotics trafficking.

His front business for drug smuggling was a high-value import house called Vantines, dealing mostly in items from Asia and receiving scant attention from customs officials. One story has it that comedienne Fanny Brice, wife of Rothstein associate Nicky Arnstein, was made to purchase items for her apartment from Vantines in order to bring in drug shipments. Rothstein had no apparent qualms about supplying narcotics to pushers and users. His philosophy was, "Look out for number one. If you don't, no one else will. If a man is dumb, someone is going to get the best of him, so why not you? If you don't, you're as dumb as he is." But while looking out for number one was what brought Arnold Rothstein to the heights of success, it is also what brought him down in the end.

A late night poker game hosted by a local gambler, George McManus, and attended by several high-stakes pros, found Rothstein in the hole to the tune of over $300,000. However, he left the table without paying up or signing any IOUs. Rothstein claimed later that the game was fixed and he wouldn't pay. After a few weeks, McManus, feeling the pressure from the other players who were owed money, arranged a meeting with Rothstein. No details of the meeting exist, but Arnold Rothstein staggered out with a gunshot in his gut. When asked who did it, he replied, "I'll take care of it." He never got the chance. He died in the hospital just a few days later. He was forty-six.

Left: Rothstein's style and poise made him the model for fictional mobsters Nathan Detroit and Meyer Wolfsheim.

Above: (Left to right) Marlon Brando, Jean Simmons, Frank Sinatra, and Vivian Blaine in the 1955 MGM release, Guys and Dolls.

Guys and Dolls

The Idyll of Miss Sarah Brown was the original story by Damon Runyon on which *Guys and Dolls* was based. Runyon was a renaissance man with a pen, working as both a sports and news reporter, playwright and an original storywriter, with over 30 movies produced based on his various works. Runyon wrote in a particular colloquial style that he picked up in the speakeasies and at the racetracks that he frequented. A man of many personal vices, Runyon hung out with many of the famous personalities of the day, including Babe Ruth, and Palm Island, Florida, neighbor, Al Capone. Another of Runyon's acquaintances was Arnold Rothstein, on whom he based the character Nathan Detroit in *Guys and Dolls*, who was played in the 1955 film by Frank Sinatra.

Dion O'Banion

"Chicago's arch criminal, who has killed or seen to the killing of at least twenty-five men."

—CHICAGO CHIEF OF POLICE MORGAN COLLINS ON DION O'BANION

He was a mobster, a killer, and a bootlegger. He had deadly feuds with the likes of Johnny Torrio and Al Capone. He owned the north side of Chicago, keeping his territory well supplied with illegal booze, and its politicians well inside his pockets. He was also the mob's florist and had a beautiful singing voice. Dion O'Banion was a man of diverse talents.

Born in Aurora, Illinois, on July 8, 1892, Dion O'Banion was still just a boy when his mother died. His father moved the small family to Chicago in 1901 and settled in a poor, largely immigrant area on the city's north side. Young Dion showed his talents as a singer in his church, performing as a choir-boy. It was also in that neighborhood where Deanie, as he was known to most, met many of his friends who would go on to be his partners in crime. There was Vincent Drucci, known as The Schemer, for all of his plots and plans. There was Earl Wajciechowski, known as Hymie Weiss, a name that flowed more easily off the tongue. And there was George Moran, known as Bugs, who had a notoriously short fuse. Together the boys made up the core of a gang that would go on to run the North Side of Chicago.

The first crimes for the burgeoning North Side Gang were simple robbery, mostly muggings and burglary. It was for burglary that Dion O'Banion did his first prison stint, for a mere three months in 1909. His second stretch in the keep came in 1911, again for a short three months, this time for carrying a gun. The two sentences would be Deanie's only time spent in prison, partly because O'Banion began making friends in high places.

In the early part of the Twentieth Century, competing newspapers fought for their turf like rival gangs, quite literally slugging it out in the streets. Young toughs found work convincing newsdealers to carry their paper exclusively, while burning rival newsstands to the ground. It was as a newspaper slugger that Dion O'Banion and his gang first began to make powerful friends, working first for the *Chicago Tribune*, and later for papers owned by William Randolph Hearst. One story tells of an official from a

Opposite: Dion O'Banion loved practical jokes and hated Italian mobsters. The mix proved deadly.

Left: The Mob's florist sports a carnation in his lapel.

Above: A crowd gathers outside Schofield's Flowers to catch a glimpse of the body of Dion O'Banion. The flower shop at 738 North State Street in Chicago also served as the headquarters of O'Banion's North Siders.

Hearst newspaper posting bail for O'Banion on a completely unrelated safe-cracking charge. It seems Deanie's services were irreplaceable.

Dion O'Banion inspired steeled loyalty among his gang mates, and seething hatred in his enemies. He was a natural leader with an easy charm and a penchant for practical jokes that weren't always so practical or funny, like getting Johnny Torrio thrown in jail. But that would come later. He also had a great love for his friends that inspired deadly revenge should any harm come to them, which extended even to the animal kingdom. One such friend, Nails Morton, was killed in a horseback riding accident. O'Banion, in his grief, reportedly responded by executing the offending horse mob-style, with a couple of bullets to the beast's head. Deanie also used to sing for his supper, working as a singing waiter in a North Side restaurant, lilting

---

VITAL SIGNS

Born: July 8, 1892
Died: November 10, 1924
Cause of Death: Murdered (shot)
Buried: Mount Carmel Cemetery; Hillside, Illinois

---

in his Irish tenor while he and his gang lightened the pockets of patrons.

Prohibition offered the North Side Gang the opportunity to move beyond the petty rackets into the riches of bootlegging. Drawing on past experience, O'Banion and his gang began their operation by hijacking other people's booze. This had the dual effect of netting a big payday for the North Siders, while making powerful enemies for O'Banion and his gang. Among his hijack victims was the deadly mob controlled by Johnny Torrio and Al Capone. Torrio had brought Capone in from New York and taken over the prostitution rackets from his uncle, Big Jim Colosimo, by assassination in 1920. The gang then quickly expanded into bootlegging as well as spreading their whorehouses around the city. But one area of the city where the houses of ill fame were not welcomed was the North Side. O'Banion, in yet another seeming contradiction, was a bootlegging, killing mobster whose Catholic faith forbade prostitution in his territory. The loss of that income combined with the booze heists didn't sit well with Torrio and Capone.

With the money generated from stealing other people's shipments, the North Siders were able to become slightly more legitimate by buying into some illegal breweries. An incident involving the Sieban Brewery may have been what finally pushed Torrio and Capone over the edge, and proved the end for Dion O'Banion. Was it one of his practical jokes? Was it his reported hatred for Italians? Whatever reasons behind his prank, it was the last one Deanie would pull.

In May of 1924, O'Banion approached Torrio with an offer. Dion told Torrio that he was getting out of the bootlegging business and wanted to liquidate his holdings. He offered to sell the Sieban Brewery for a decent price, and Torrio leapt at the chance to move into the North Side. One version of the story has O'Banion delivering a personal tour of the facilities to Torrio when the cops raided the place and arrested both men. O'Banion was released with a fine as a first time offender of Prohibition laws. Torrio, as a second offender, was given a prison sentence. One version of the story holds that O'Banion had purposely tipped off the cops before the sale. Another maintains that O'Banion merely knew the raid was going to happen and saw an opportunity to cash in. Either way, Torrio had been set up, was on his way to jail, and Deanie was laughing all the way to the bank with a reported $500,000 for the sale of the now worthless brewery.

Both Johnny Torrio and Al Capone wanted to hit O'Banion. But, as reports go, one man stood in their way. As head of the Chicago chapter of the Unione Siciliane, Mike Merlo was a powerful man. The Unione Siciliane was a fraternal order of Sicilians that, in addition to advocating for and aiding Italian immigrants, was also mostly run and populated by mobsters of Sicilian descent. The society had chapters across the country, and as a result, pulled a lot of weight, given the combined clout and muscle of its membership. In 1924, Mike Merlo was dying of cancer and was in a relatively peaceable mood. Merlo reportedly sought to avoid a gang war while he still lived and vetoed Torrio's request to hit O'Banion. Torrio bided his time. Merlo's days were numbered. So were Deanie's.

Prohibition also allowed Dion O'Banion to indulge in one of his other loves: flowers. O'Banion not only owned a flower shop, Schofield's Flowers on North State Street, but he also worked in the shop, lovingly building arrangements, often for the funerals of fellow mobsters. The death of Mike Merlo on November 8, 1924, brought a lot of business to Schofield's Flowers. On the day of the funeral, November 10, 1924, three men walked into the shop. O'Banion may have thought they were there to pick up an order for the Merlo funeral. Perhaps it was the way they were dressed or carried

themselves. Probably without suspicion, Deanie reportedly reached out a friendly hand to one of the men who immediately clamped his grip on the Irish mobster's mitt as his accomplices produced guns and began shooting. When they walked out, Dion O'Banion lay dead on the floor of his flower shop, shot twice in chest, twice in the neck, and twice in the face.

Reports differ, but it is largely believed that the shooters were Capone killers Albert Anselmi and John Scalise, while the man glad-handing O'Banion was Frankie Yale, an old friend of Torrio's and Capone's from New York. (Capone would later have all three killed, personally beating Scalise and Anselmi to death with a baseball bat.) The war that ensued after O'Banion's murder would culminate in the St. Valentine's Day Massacre, an ironic legacy for the mob's florist.

Below: Police search for evidence at the scene of O'Banion's murder inside Schofield's Flowers. O'Banion, ironically, had been preparing flowers for a fellow mobster's funeral when he was gunned down.

Vincent "Mad Dog" Coll

"Five planes brought dozens of machine gats from Chicago Friday to combat The Town's Capone. Local banditti have made one hotel a virtual arsenal and several hot spots are ditto because Master Coll is giving them the headache."

—Walter Winchell newspaper column, February 8, 1932

It takes a special kind of man to make his living ripping off and kidnapping mobsters. Such a man would have to be audacious, daring, and a maybe a bit psychotic. Such a man was Vincent "Mad Dog" Coll. Coll made a significant amount of money kidnapping mobsters for ransom. That sort of stunt may have been feasible before the Castellammarese War, but after Salvatore Maranzano and Joe Masseria were dead, Lucky Luciano and Meyer Lansky wanted to do things differently. And differently meant disparate gangs working together for their common good instead of killing each other and causing a ruckus in the press. Mad Dog Coll couldn't adapt to the new way of working. He had to go.

Vincent Coll was born in Ireland in 1908 and emigrated to New York with his family to settle in a heavily Irish section of Manhattan known as Hell's Kitchen. Coll grew up like so many other hoodlums of the time, making a living with petty theft and terrorizing street vendors. But Coll was always willing to go the extra mile when it came to the use of violence, a quality that landed him a job with bootlegger Dutch Schultz. Their relationship soon soured, however, when Coll sought to become more than a rumrunner and gunsel for Schultz. He wanted an equal cut of the profits. Schultz scoffed at the youngster and in the process bought himself a big Irish headache

In his twenty-three years, Vincent Coll managed to make himself a headache to many in the underworld. He had a running hit-for-hit war going with Schultz (which resulted in the death of Coll's brother, Peter, and some twenty others on both sides), he was kidnapping for ransom mobsters close to Legs Diamond and Owney Madden, and he was staging heists of mob track money. Perhaps it was this audacity and apparent death wish that caught the eye of Salvatore Maranzano.

Maranzano was in the market for a hitman for a very special job. He had seemingly just won his war with "Joe the Boss" Masseria for control of the mob, and was looking to shore up his power to become the mob's *capo di tutti capo,* the boss of all bosses. He knew that Charles "Lucky" Luciano had ambitions of seizing control of the underworld, and Maranzano decided to make sure that those ambitions were never realized. And to be safe, he wanted the other young guns taken out too, including Frank Costello, Vito Genovese, and Joe Adonis.

Opposite: A nationwide manhunt was issued for Vincent Coll's capture in connection with the shooting death of a child in Harlem in 1931. This retouched photo along with a description of the "Mad Mick" was distributed throughout the country.

Above: Vincent Coll's gang lines up for this photo taken at police headquarters the day after they were captured in connection with the "Baby Killer" shootings. (Left to right) Dominick Ordierno, Pasquale Del Greco, Mike Baisle, Frank Giordano and Vincent Coll. Detectives are in the rear.

Such a hit would require a special brand of fearless psychosis. Maranzano called on the "Mad Mick."

A deal was reportedly struck between Maranzano and Coll for the hit and a down payment of $25,000 was exchanged. Lucky Luciano, however, was a step ahead of Maranzano. On September 10, 1931, Maranzano was shot and stabbed to death in his office. The contract between the men dissolved with Maranzano's

--- **VITAL SIGNS** ---

Born: July 20, 1908
Died: February 8, 1932
Cause of Death: Murdered (shot)
Buried: St. Raymond's Cemetery; Bronx, New York

death. Coll opted out of the hit, but kept the twenty-five grand anyway.

Meanwhile, Coll's war with Dutch Schultz continued. It was the newspapers that gave Vincent the nickname "Mad Dog" when on July 28, 1931, Coll, who was gunning for one of Schultz's men, Joey Rao, killed a child and wounded four others. There were many witnesses to the shooting and it wasn't long before Mad Dog Coll was on trial for the murder of a five-year-old boy. One story tells of Coll kidnapping Owney Madden's right-hand man, George Jean "Big Frenchy" DeManage, to raise enough money for a good lawyer. In the end he was well represented by Samuel Leibowitz—despite all the evidence and witnesses against him, Mad Dog Coll was acquitted.

But the press was filled with stories about the "baby killer," and such reports were bad for business. Vincent Coll had worn out his welcome. The mob had a handsome ransom on Coll's head, and it was only a matter of time before someone collected.

Collection day was February 8, 1932. The place was a phone booth in a drug store on West 23rd Street in Manhattan. Coll was reportedly on the phone with Owney Madden, threatening him with violence for money, when three men stepped out of a car and opened fire on the booth with Tommy guns, killing Coll instantly. The shooters were never identified. Any number of mobsters (and policemen and private citizens, for that matter) would have had reason to call the hit. No one would miss Vincent Coll.

Legal Eagle

Mad Dog Coll's lawyer, Samuel S. Leibowitz, is probably best known for his involvement in the Scottsboro trial. In 1931, nine black men were convicted of raping two white women in Alabama and were sentenced to death. Their case was appealed by the International Labor Defense to the Supreme Court, which ruled that the nine men had not received an adequate defense. The high profile defense attorney Samuel Leibowitz was called in from New York to represent the nine men. One of Leibowitz's first actions was to set up grounds for appeal by showing that blacks had been purposely kept off Alabama jury rolls. Ultimately, after many years, several more convictions, death sentences and subsequent appeals, none of the men was put to death. Leibowitz returned to New York having changed his reputation from defender of baby killers to defender of civil rights.

Left: A detective points out bullet holes in the phone booth inside the London Chemist drug store on Twenty-third Street near Eighth Avenue where Vincent Coll had been talking on the phone when he was gunned down.

Above: Samuel Leibowitz shares a smoke with some of the defendants in the Scottsboro trial in 1937. (Left to right) Willie Robertson, Eugene Williams, Samuel Leibowitz, Roy Wright, Olen Montgomery.

Jack "Legs" Diamond

"Three times in the last four years his enemies tried to put him on the spot. Each time Legs went to a hospital. Each time he cheated death. But after his last miraculous recovery it was declared that his body was so full of lead that it would sink in Salt Lake."
—*Daily News,* SATURDAY, DECEMBER 19, 1931

By many accounts, Jack "Legs" Diamond wasn't well liked by anybody. If the amount of times he was shot is any indication, those accounts are true. Diamond survived no fewer than four near-fatal shootings, earning a reputation of "clay pigeon of the underworld." He was unaffiliated with any of New York's crime families, and so felt no loyalty to anyone. In the world of the mob, however, a man without loyalty to anyone is a danger to everyone. Throughout his career in crime, Legs Diamond routinely sold out friends and partners in his drive for money and power. A man like that couldn't evade the assassin's bullet forever.

Early accounts of Diamond's life are sketchy. He was born in 1897 and had one brother, Eddie. Jack began as a petty thief, where he reportedly earned the nickname "Legs" for his ability to successfully elude the cops (although, based on photographs, it could just as easily have been in reference to his long legs). He came into the employ of labor racketeer and bootlegger, Jacob "Little Augie" Orgen, working as a bodyguard and enforcer. In 1927 Little Augie was reluctant to expand his business and some of his underlings became impatient. During

a successful hit attempt on Little Augie, Legs Diamond was wounded. Legs recognized Louis "Lepke" Buchalter, another of Orgen's own men, as one of the hitmen. It is likely that a deal was struck between the two men, for Lepke soon took over his former boss's labor rackets, while Diamond himself, moved in on Little Augie's bootlegging business.

Opposite: *Jack "Legs" Diamond in a 1930 mug shot. At the time of this photo he had already survived three separate shootings.*

Left: *Jacob "Little Augie" Orgen in 1927, the year he was murdered. Jack Diamond had been acting as Orgen's bodyguard at the time and sustained several bullet wounds for his trouble.*

Above: Jack Diamond enters courthouse in Troy, New York, in 1931. He was later acquitted of the charges of kidnapping the driver of a rival bootlegger's truck.

guard and bouncer in his gambling houses and also reportedly helped fund Diamond in his bootlegging business. Legs was upwardly mobile, however, and their association was short lived, with reports of a feud between the two men. Diamond wanted to be in charge, not just a hired gun.

Diamond opened his own joint, The Hotsy Totsy Club in Manhattan. The club was also the headquarters for his crime operation, and reportedly a place to take care of the competition. A rival mobster might enter the club for a meeting with Diamond, and leave as a corpse. In 1929, one such corpse belonged to a street hood named Red Cassidy. At the bar, Diamond shot Cassidy in the head, in front of witnesses. When the police came looking for Legs, he went into hiding, only to turn himself in after several Hotsy Totsy employees and patrons turned up either dead or missing. With no witnesses to his involvement in the murder of Cassidy or anyone else, no charges were brought against him.

But Diamond's time in hiding gave rival mobster Dutch Schultz the opportunity to move in on Legs' bootlegging business. A turf war ensued between the two men. Before this time, Diamond had survived two separate shooting incidents, once taking some buckshot to the head. The war between Legs and Schultz would add some more holes to Diamond's body.

Schultz was seeking revenge for the murder of two of his men when, in October of 1930, gunmen entered Legs' hotel suite and fatally shot him. Or so

At this time Diamond came into contact with another early influence, mobster and gambler Arnold Rothstein. Rothstein employed Diamond as a body-

— VITAL SIGNS —

Born: 1897
Died: December 17, 1931
Cause of Death: Murdered (shot)
Buried: Mount Olivet Cemetery; Queens, New York

— SCREEN TIME —

Murder, Inc. (1960). Played by Richard Everhart (with Peter Falk as Kid "Twist" Reles)
The Rise & Fall of Legs Diamond (1960). Played by Ray Danton

they thought. Diamond's showgirl love interest, Kiki Roberts, had been with him in the room when he was shot, but she was unharmed. Kiki had Legs rushed to the hospital where he miraculously survived. Only a few months later another attempt on his life gained Legs four more holes in his body. Again, he survived.

Perhaps thinking himself immortal, Diamond foolishly announced that he was seeking revenge against Schultz, and, as a threat to New York's crime families, he was also looking to expand his territory. Legs had taken the wrong lessons away from all of his brushes with death. Instead of interpreting the many attempts on his life as a sign that he should retire quietly, he grew emboldened and arrogant, and it was that hubris that finally brought him down.

Whoever shot Legs Diamond in a hotel room in Albany, New York, in December of 1931, made sure "the clay pigeon of the underworld" wouldn't survive. Burn marks indicated that a gun was held to his head when three bullets were fired, finally killing Jack "Legs" Diamond. Some say it was Dutch Schultz settling the score. Some say it was the Syndicate protecting their interests. Some say it was the cops who were fed up with the killer who would not die. Whoever it was, they finally got it right.

Above: One of the last photographs of Legs Diamond taken in a courtroom following his acquittal on kidnapping charges on October 18, 1931. Diamond was gunned down in a hotel room several hours later. Defense lawyer Daniel A. Prior shakes hands with Diamond's wife, Alice. Legs is second from the right as defense staff looks on.

It's a Tough Job...

After Legs Diamond failed to guard Little Augie Orgen's body from Louis Lepke and Gurrah Shapiro, he wisely got out of the labor slugging business. As the name suggests, labor slugging was a violent way to make a living. Orgen had taken over his garment district labor rackets by masterminding the murder of Nathan "Kid Dropper" Kaplan. At the time of his death in 1923, Kid Dropper was one of the more powerful criminals in New York City. He, of course, had attained that position by masterminding the murder of competitor and one-time partner Johnny Spanish. One apocryphal story of their falling out describes Spanish's pregnant girlfriend dumping him for Kid Dropper. In a fit of jealously and rage, Spanish shot the woman in the abdomen. She survived and gave birth to an otherwise healthy baby who was missing several fingers that had been shot off.

Above: The bustling Manhattan Garment District in 1943.

Bugs Moran

"…when the killing took place the persons actually perpetrating therein did not know the identity of each of their victims but rather than risk the possibility of missing [Bugs] Moran, killed all of the persons found in the garage."

—Excerpt of August 27, 1936, letter From J. Edgar Hoover to Attorney General Joseph B. Keenan regarding the St. Valentine's Day Massacre

The single most infamous mob hit in American history was ultimately a colossal failure. The hit that would come to be called the St. Valentine's Day Massacre killed seven men, none of whom was the principal target. George "Bugs" Moran was running late that day.

Born to a Polish mother and Irish father, George Clarence Moran came into the world in rural Minnesota in 1893. His parents moved to the north side of Chicago around the turn of the century in hopes of finding steady work in the teeming city. But work in the Irish slums of Chicago was hard to come by and paid little. The young George Moran decided against breaking his back for peanuts and began stealing horses and holding them for ransom. Spinning in similar, lawless circles, it wasn't long before Moran met and teamed up with another fellow Irish hooligan, Dion O'Banion. O'Banion was a natural and charismatic leader who inspired loyalty and trust in those under him, regardless of ethnicity or religion. He led a gang of boys who called themselves the North Side Gang, which included Moran and trusted lieutenants, Hymie Weiss and Vincent "The Schemer" Drucci.

Petty crime, mostly robbery and some extortion, was the order of the day for the teens. In 1912, a North Siders' robbery of a warehouse went bad and the nineteen-year-old Bugs was nabbed by the cops. Moran kept silent about who his accomplices were and was sentenced to two years at Joliet State Prison. When he was released in 1914, Bugs was welcomed back into the North Side Gang, who were grateful for his having taken the fall without squealing. A premium was placed on that loyalty, an all-for-one mentality that would eventually lead to the demise of the gang itself.

Opposite: Bugs Moran poses for a photo circa 1931, two years after the massacre that sought his life.

Below: The morning after: A crowd gathers to watch as bodies are removed from the rear of 2122 North Clark Street on February 15, 1929.

On the eve of Prohibition, the North Side Gang had expanded into other areas of crime, including work as newspaper enforcers, collecting a fee from city newspapers to ensure that newsstands would not carry rival papers. Also at this time, O'Banion was working in a restaurant as a singing waiter, entertaining patrons with popular Irish tunes as Bugs Moran and his fellow North Siders picked the pockets of diners. Another endeavor for the gang was ensuring that the right people got elected to government posts, the right people being those who would pay the most to have the ballot boxes stuffed in their favor. In the criminal world, it always paid to have friends in high places, and politicians in your pocket.

Despite his burgeoning political connections, Bugs was sent back to Joliet in 1917 for the armed robbery of a department store, this time for a five-year stint. When Moran returned to his North Siders in 1923, he found a country wrestling with Prohibition, and his old friends awash with cash from the bootlegging of illicit alcohol. O'Banion and

the gang had managed to claim the North Side of Chicago as their territory and collected on every drop of liquor and beer consumed within its boundaries. Bugs fell right back in with his old mates, reaping vast sums of money from rumrunning during the dry years. The old North Side Gang was back together again. But not for long.

Johnny Torrio and his underboss, Al Capone, were attempting to take over all bootlegging operations in Chicago, including the North Side. Standing in the way of their dominance was Dion O'Banion, Bugs Moran, and the North Siders. On November 10, 1924, Torrio/Capone men gunned down O'Banion in the gang's headquarters, O'Banion's own flower shop. What followed was an all-out gang war carried out on the streets and throughout the neighborhoods of Chicago.

On January 12, 1925 the North Siders made a hit attempt on Capone in a Prohibition era drive-by shooting. Tommy guns blazed from the running boards of passing cars, with Bugs Moran leading the way. Capone survived unhurt, thrown to the ground by his bodyguard behind his own car. Less than two weeks later, the North Siders tried to put a hit on Torrio, with somewhat more success. One version tells of Hymie Weiss shotgunning Torrio to the ground. Then Bugs Moran placed his revolver to Torrio's temple and pulled the trigger, only to have the gun misfire. The commotion aroused by the shooting prevented the job from being finished. Torrio survived, but quickly retired, leaving the business to Capone.

On September 20, 1926, the North Siders made a second attempt at Capone, this time at Capone's hotel headquarters. The technique was the same. Cars rolled by with Tommy guns blazing into the ground floor of the hotel, and yielding the same result: Capone was again unhurt. Miraculously, neither was anyone else, despite the more than 1,000 rounds fired.

The next casualty in the war was Hymie Weiss, who was gunned down in October of 1926. Then Vinnie Drucci stepped in as leader of the North Siders,

Left: Earl Wajciechowski, aka Hymie Weiss, a native of Poland, wasn't Jewish as his nickname might suggest, but rather a devout Catholic. It's not clear how he got the moniker.

only to be shot to death by cops six months later. The only original O'Banion lieutenant left was Bugs Moran.

George Moran was generally well-liked, for a mobster. He had a keen sense of humor and was always good for a juicy quote to newspapermen, sometimes slyly admitting his guilt to reporters after acquittals, and sharing jokes with judges

Left: Bugs Moran (center) and Frank Parker (seated at right) surrounded by defense team while on trial for conspiracy to forge and counterfeit $62,000 worth of money orders. The amount was petty in comparison to what Moran had made during Prohibition.

Right: The brothers Gusenberg: Frank (left) and Peter, both victims of the St. Valentine's Day Massacre. Frank lived for several hours after being shot. When asked who shot him, he reportedly replied, "I ain't no copper."

about his criminal activities. He was also a devoted Catholic, refusing to allow prostitution in his territory. He was often the preferred bootlegger, relatively speaking, to Capone who was becoming distrusted and feared among officials and the general public. And the two mobsters reportedly had an intense hatred for one another, a hatred constantly fueled by

the very personal gang war. Something had to give. As the cliché goes, the town wasn't big enough for the both of them. On St. Valentine's Day, 1929, Capone made his move.

The plan was simple and seemed to go off without a hitch. Some of Capone's men, posing as independent hijackers, offered a load of "stolen" whiskey to Bugs Moran at a price he couldn't refuse. They scheduled to drop the load off at Moran's headquarters, an innocuous looking garage on North Clark Street called the S-M-C Cartage Company, acting as a front for the North Siders' rum-running business. At the appointed hour, with Bugs and his men assembled and waiting for the shipment, the garage was raided by Capone men dressed as cops. The bootleggers dutifully complied with the order to line up against the wall. How could they know they were lining up for their own executions? The Tommy guns and shotguns blazed and when the smoke cleared, the fake cops split the scene, leaving six men dead inside the garage. The seventh, Frank Gusenberg, died the next day. The only hitch in the plan was that Bugs Moran

---

—— VITAL SIGNS ——

Born: 1893
Died: February 25, 1957
Cause of Death: Natural causes (lung cancer)
Buried: Cemetery of Leavenworth Penitentiary; Leavenworth, Kansas

---

—— SCREEN TIME ——

The St. Valentine's Day Massacre (1967). Played by Ralph Meeker (with Jason Robards as Al Capone)
Al Capone (1959). Played by Murvyn Vye (with Rod Steiger as Al Capone)

Macabre Memorabilia

had been running late and never made it to the fateful lineup. The hit had missed its mark.

The public outrage that the St. Valentine's Day Massacre sparked lit a fire under local and federal officials. The gang war had to stop, one way or another. It was federal prosecutors who ended the war by putting Al Capone in prison for tax evasion. But Bugs Moran fared little better. His gang decimated by the war, his territory lost to Capone forces, and public opinion turned against the feuding mobsters, Moran eventually left Chicago and attempted to regain his former wealth and power by robbing banks and stores throughout the Midwest. He was caught and convicted of one such robbery in Ohio in 1946, and was sent to Leavenworth for ten years. Immediately upon his release he was convicted of another, previous bank robbery, and sent back to Leavenworth where he died an ignominious death of lung cancer on February 25, 1957. The former leader of the North Side Gang, who had once warred with Al Capone, was buried in a pauper's grave just outside the prison walls.

Above: The U.S. Federal Penitentiary in Leavenworth, Kansas.

Above, right: The scene of the St. Valentine's Day Massacre, February 14, 1929. The bricks of the wall can now be purchased online.

In a bizarre and macabre side note, the 414 bricks that made up the back wall of 2122 North Clark Street, and subsequently the backstop for the firing squad's bullets in the St. Valentine's Day Massacre, have gone on to inspire their own mythology.

As the story goes, a Canadian man bought the entire wall in 1967, individually numbered each brick, then dismantled the wall and had it shipped to Vancouver, B.C. Since that time, the wall has been displayed in different locations (once reportedly behind Plexiglas as a sort of backstop in the men's room of a bar), and there have also been attempts to sell it. There was a deal to sell the wall in its entirety to a casino in Las Vegas, but that was reportedly shot down. Since that time, separate bricks have gone on sale (for as much as $1000 a pop), individually numbered, complete with a descriptive plaque.

Urban legend has it that those who own one of the Massacre bricks can expect bad luck to befall them, replete with visits from the ghosts of slain mobsters. Currently, photos of bricks purported to be authentic can be found proudly displayed on Internet sites as macabre pieces of memorabilia from that most famous of massacres on St. Valentine's Day of 1929.

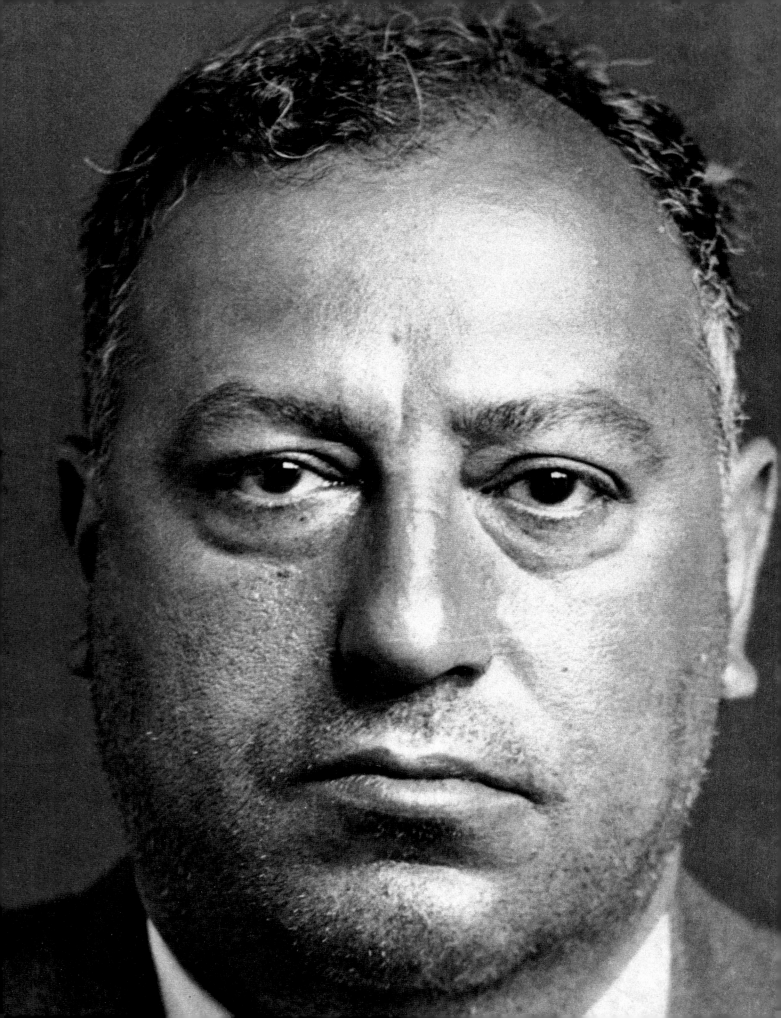

Waxey Gordon

"You have demonstrated repeatedly that there is no crime or racket to which you would not resort in order to make a dollar. Your latest and most dastardly offense is typical of your hostility and it should bring down the curtain on your parasitic and lawless life."
—JUDGE FRANCIS L. VELENTE,
SENTENCING WAXEY GORDON TO TWENTY-FIVE YEARS TO LIFE IN PRISON

For various reasons, the Feds had difficulty convicting mobsters for much of anything. Usually witnesses of mob crimes would change testimony, disappear, or turn up dead. Evidence would vanish. Juries and judges would be paid off. Stool pigeons would attempt to fly. Convicting mobsters was just plain difficult. So federal prosecutors tried a different, and largely successful tactic, of prosecuting mobsters for income tax evasion, where convictions were not based on any one piece of evidence, but rather a wide and varying body of evidence, which was difficult to dispose of. Such is the case of Irving Wexler. But much of the evidence used against Wexler was supplied by an unlikely source: rival mobsters.

Irving Wexler was born in New York in 1888 to Polish-Jewish parents. He was raised on Manhattan's Lower East Side, soon taking the alias Waxey Gordon. The nickname "Waxey" apparently came from his prowess at pickpocketing goods as if they were covered with wax. Early on he joined the Dopey Benny Fein Gang, which specialized in labor rackets. In 1914, a series of arrests for assault, robbery and murder sent Gordon to Sing Sing for two years. Upon his release he

began working for gambler and underworld financier, Arnold Rothstein, who played a major role in nuturing a generation of mobsters. In 1920 Gordon approached Rothstein for financial backing of a bootlegging scheme to smuggle illicit alcohol from Great Britain. Rothstein was not actively involved in the rumrunning business, but rather funded mobsters like Gordon in the

Opposite: A 1933 mug shot of Irving Wexler, aka Waxey Gordon, after his arrest in North White Lake, New York. Gordon had been on the lam from federal authorities who sought an indictment on tax evasion charges.

Left: Waxey Gordon calmly lights a cigar outside the courtroom just prior to being sentenced to ten years in prison and an $80,000 fine for tax evasion.

Right: Thomas E. Dewey as a crusading prosecutor in 1937. Dewey went on to be governor of New York and ran for president of the United States in 1948, losing narrowly to Harry S. Truman. The race was close enough for the Chicago Daily Tribune *to put out a premature edition proclaiming the famous headline,* "Dewey Defeats Truman."

endeavor. This arrangement allowed Waxey to build a very successful bootlegging business.

In 1925 a disgruntled ship captain in Gordon's smuggling fleet decided to blow the whistle on Waxey's operations. Gordon's Manhattan headquarters were raided and his equipment seized, including trucks and boats. Before Gordon could be prosecuted, however, the ship captain mysteriously died in police custody, and the investigation was dropped. But with his operation exposed and equipment confiscated, Waxey left New York and relocated to New Jersey and expanded his bootlegging business into Philadelphia, Pennsylvania.

── VITAL SIGNS ──

Born: January 19, 1888
Died: June 24, 1952
Cause of Death: Natural causes (heart attack)
Buried: Mount Hebron Cemetery; Queens, New York

It was in New Jersey that Waxey Gordon had a fateful interaction with mobster Meyer Lansky that would be the beginning of what would later become known as the "War of the Jews." In truth, it wasn't much of a war, but the winner was clear. In 1928 several of Waxey's men were killed when one of his booze shipments was hijacked enroute to Philadelpia. Meyer Lansky was recognized as one of the hijackers. Gordon sought revenge. But a mob war was not included in the plans of Lansky and Lucky Luciano, who sought to build a national crime syndicate. They decided to rid themselves of the problem that was Waxey Gordon, but agreed not to remove him with a bullet to the head, which might spark war and retaliation. Instead, Lansky and Luciano quietly fed information of Gordon's finances to prosecutors. The information provided fuel to Waxey's prosecution on tax evasion charges.

The prosecutor in the case was the energetic crusader Thomas E. Dewey, who with a team of investigators, worked tirelessly on the case for two years. At times, investigators seeking to review bank records would be made to wait until some of Gordon's men showed up and removed the documents. On one occasion, investigators were actually arrested in Hoboken and held by local police long enough for evidence against Waxey to go missing. But Dewey and his investigators persevered, and with the help of Lansky and Luciano, eventually turned up extensive evidence showing Gordon's claim of $8,100 in income in 1930 to be understated to the tune of over two million dollars. The jury took less than an hour to convict. In December of 1933, Waxey Gordon was sentenced to ten years in prison and an $80,000 fine.

Gordon was released from Leavenworth in 1940 after having served seven years of his sentence. He emerged from the penitentiary saying, "Waxey Gordon is dead. From now on, it's Irving Wexler, salesman." However, Waxey neglected to elaborate on what exactly he would be selling. A decade later, Irving Wexler was indeed a salesman, but his arrest on August 2, 1951, was for selling heroin. Upon his release from prison in 1940, Waxey set about building a national narcotics ring. He was found guilty of narcotics trafficking, and due in part to his previous criminal record, was sentenced to twenty-five years to life. A life sentence is what it was. On June 24, 1952, while awaiting trial on additional drug trafficking charges, Gordon suffered a massive heart attack in an Alcatraz infirmary. He died immediately. There were reports that Irving Wexler was about to turn state evidence in order to reduce his sentence. The mobster who was sold up the river by rivals so many years earlier, was apparently looking to do some selling of his own.

Left: Waxey Gordon leaving New York police headquarters after questioning in 1933.

Above: So close and yet so far: Alcatraz as seen in 1950 in the middle of San Francisco Bay with the city itself in the background, just out of reach.

The Rock

Easily the most famous of all prisons, Alcatraz had a surprisingly short history as a federal penitentiary, spanning less than thirty years. The oral history of American Indians who lived in the San Francisco Bay area some 15,000 years ago suggests that the island was sometimes used as a place for ostracized tribe members. In the mid-1800s, the island became a U.S. military fortress, boasting the first lighthouse on the Pacific coast. During the American Civil War the Union military realized the usefulness of Alcatraz as a prison, housing the crew of a Confederate privateer ship. The island again served as a military prison during the Spanish-American War. In the early 1930s, the Federal Bureau of Prisons was looking to create a special prison that would essentially be reserved for racketeers and other difficult and predatory criminals who presumably could not be rehabilitated. In 1934, the bureau settled on Alcatraz as the location for its special prison. Over the years "The Rock," as it became known, grew in legend, hosting such guests as Waxey Gordon, Al Capone, George "Machine Gun" Kelly, Mickey Cohen, and Robert Franklin Stroud, famously known as the "Birdman of Alcatraz." Alcatraz was closed as a federal prison in 1963, due to its considerable operation costs, having been home to some 1,545 prisoners over its twenty-nine years.

Frankie Yale

"Presidents are buried with less to-do."

—A New York newspaper's account of the funeral of Frankie Yale

In Gangland, everything that comes around goes around. A wrong done to a mobster, even a close friend, was sure to bring retribution. Such is the tale of Frankie Yale, a Brooklyn mobster who mentored a young Alphonse Capone and later ended up dead by his apprentice's hand.

Francesco Ioele was born in Italy, in 1893. Known on the streets of his adopted New York for his quick temper and propensity towards violence, Frankie Yale (sometimes Uale) was not to be messed with. In Brooklyn, he met and teamed up with Johnny Torrio, forming the Five Points Gang, named after their Brooklyn neighborhood. The gang specialized in extortion rackets called the Black Hand, one that preyed on the immigrant population in the neighborhood, usually recent arrivals too frightened to complain to the police. The Black Hand was a simple intimidation racket, imported from Italy, in which immigrants received letters that threatened violence if money was not immediately forthcoming. The letters were signed with a simple black hand print. The scheme was used by a great many unaffiliated gangs, which often gave the impression of a vast criminal network. Occasionally, those who did not pay were beaten or killed to set an example to others who sought to ignore the Black Hand. Yale was especially good at dealing with those who would not pay up.

Yale's legitimate business was a restaurant called the Harvard Inn. Ever on the lookout for young toughs willing to do odd jobs such as tending bar, waiting tables, breaking a few arms, Yale hired an eighteen-year-old Al Capone at Torrio's suggestion. Working as a bartender and bouncer, it was at the Harvard Inn that Capone received his nickname. After an ill-conceived attempt to woo the sister of local mobster Frank Gallucio, a fight ensued in which Capone walked away with several nasty knife lacerations on his face, the scars of which he would bear for the rest of his life, as well as the apropos moniker, "Scarface." Frankie Yale reportedly had to smooth over the situation with Gallucio's boss, Lucky Luciano, making the young Capone apologize for his rudeness. Yale tried to impress upon Capone that violence was a great means of getting what you want, but there was a time to fight and a time to make peace. It was a lesson Capone had trouble learning.

Torrio left for Chicago in 1915 to help out his uncle, Big Jim Colosimo, Chicago's biggest purveyor of whorehouses, who was being squeezed by mobsters trying to horn in on his business. Yale was now the lone head of the Five Points Gang. Not long after, Capone followed Torrio to Chicago, due in part to some pesky murder charges pending against him. One version of events has it that when Prohibition

Opposite: Frankie Yale poses in his best pinstripes in 1928.

Right: A police officer stands guard at the scene of Yale's murder on 44th Street in Brooklyn, New York. Among the possessions found on the body were a diamond stickpin and a diamond-studded belt buckle.

came, Colosimo was reluctant to get into the business of rumrunning, preferring the comfort and ease of his nightclubs and whorehouses. Frustrated by the shortsightedness of his boss, Torrio decided that a change was necessary. It is generally believed that Torrio called in his friend and old partner, Frankie Yale, to help. A waiter at Colosimo's Café thought he recognized Yale as the man who shot his boss to death on May 11, 1920, but for some reason he refused to testify in court. With Colosimo out of the way, Torrio took over his business, and with newly promoted underboss, Capone, at his side, he expanded into the business of bootlegging.

Yale, meanwhile, greatly expanded his bootlegging business in Brooklyn during Prohibition. He headed the national Unione Siciliane, and also became heavily involved in tobacco rackets. But despite his business success, Yale never lost his taste for blood. His talents were needed by Torrio only a few years after the Colosimo killing to clean up a dispute with rival bootlegger, Dion O'Banion. The unpredictable O'Banion had it in for Torrio, even setting him up for a fall by selling him a brewery that he knew was about to be raided. On the morning of November 10, 1924, three men, including Frankie Yale, walked into O'Banion's flower store. One particularly colorful version of the story has Yale greeting O'Banion with a hearty handshake, his grip not releasing until O'Banion was dead from multiple gunshot wounds courtesy of Yale's companions.

The murder of their beloved leader brought the wrath of O'Banion's gang down on the heads of Torrio and Capone. In 1925, after a nearly successful attempt on his life, Torrio decided to call it quits, and handed the business over to Capone. Capone was having trouble with his whiskey supply, so he cut a deal with his former mentor in New York, Frankie Yale, to supply him with the booze.

After a few too many of those shipments were hijacked, Capone became suspicious, and sent a mole to spy on Yale. His suspicions were confirmed. Yale was hijacking his own paid shipments bound for Capone, then selling them back to Scarface. There is speculation that Yale was staging these heists to compensate for dues that Capone was refusing to pay to the Unione Siciliane, as well as to pressure Scarface Al into paying those dues. Although Yale found out he had a mole in his midst and had him killed, he was too late. Capone knew about the double cross. Yale's one-time pupil knew what had to be done.

On July 1, 1928, Yale was ambushed while driving on a Brooklyn street by some of Capone's men, who forced his car to the side of the road and began shooting. Yale's car and body were rid-dled with bullets, killing him instantly. One of the guns recovered from the scene was a Thompson submachine gun, the popular weapon of choice among Chicago's mobs. Frankie Yale had the dubious honor of being the first mobster in New York whacked with a Tommy gun.

Yale's funeral was truly a spectacle, after the mobster's own wishes to have the biggest and best mob burial. A reported 10,000 mourners were present along the funeral procession route and at Holy Cross Cemetery in Brooklyn. In the procession itself were 250 cars, including 38 carloads of flowers, all following the $15,000 nickel and silver coffin. Also present were two women who could each legally claim to be Yale's wife. It seemed only fitting that the mobster who had been responsible for so many mob funerals had the most grandiose gangland sendoff of all.

Below: Frankie Yale's coffin is placed on the hearse that will bear it to the cemetery as thousands vie for a glimpse of the spectacle.

Al Capone

"This American system of ours—call it Americanism, call is capitalism, call it what you like—gives to each and every one of us a great opportunity if we only seize it with both hands and make the most of it."
—AL CAPONE

Easily the best-known mobster of all time, Al Capone's short reign as head of the Chicago Outfit was characterized by brutality and mayhem. Between 1925 and 1932, Capone waged war against rival gangs on the streets of the Windy City, culminating in a brutal slaughter of rival mobsters known as the St. Valentine's Day Massacre. Over the years, film and television have presented an image of Capone that was seemingly larger than life. This is only fitting, because in his heyday, Al Capone *was* larger than life.

Alphonse Capone was born in Brooklyn, New York, on January 17, 1899. A middle child in a large family, Al grew up in the poverty of the immigrant ghettos. He found early camaraderie in some of the youth gangs in the neighborhood, then later became involved with the Five Points Gang, led by Johnny Torrio and Frankie Yale. Capone quit school at the age of fourteen after he supposedly won a fistfight with a female teacher, then lost one to the male school principal. He eventually landed a job at Frankie Yale's Harvard Inn in Coney Island. Working as a bartender and bouncer, it was at the Harvard Inn that Al Capone would get his infamous nickname, "Scarface." However, Al's friends, for reasons unknown, called him "Snorky," a nickname decidedly lacking in dramatic flare.

In 1919, Torrio brought Capone out west to help out in Chicago. The two tried to convince Torrio's uncle, Big Jim Colosimo, to expand his prostitution rackets into the bigger business of rumrunning. When Colosimo refused, Torrio and Capone knocked him off in his own

Opposite: Al Capone smiling and smoking aboard a train carrying him to the federal penitentiary in Atlanta to begin serving his eleven-year sentence for tax evasion.

Left: Capone in a 1925 Chicago police photograph.

Right: Capone in his finest duds stares into camera in this undated photo.

Below: "Pappa Johnny" Torrio in 1931. The mobster supposedly retired after a near fatal shooting in 1925, but kept active as a sort of elder statesman and general consigliere to the mob until his death of a heart attack in a barber chair in 1957.

Dion O'Banion was killed in his own flower shop in November 1924; many say it was the handiwork of Frankie Yale again. O'Banion's gang vowed revenge on both Torrio and Capone. Retaliation came on January 12, 1925, when some North Siders, now led by Hymie Weiss, staged a drive-by shooting aimed at Capone. On his way to dinner in a downtown Chicago restaurant, Al had just stepped out of his limousine when shots rang out from a passing car. Capone's bodyguard had pushed Capone to the sidewalk and he survived the attack, unhurt. Less than two weeks later, an attempt on Johnny Torrio was more successful, leaving Torrio clinging to life. He eventually recovered, but badly shaken by the event, Torrio decided to retire and leave the business to Capone. There have been claims made that it was actually Capone who put the hit out on Johnny Torrio, just as Torrio had done to Big Jim Colosimo five years earlier, but there is little evidence to support this claim. In 1925, Al Capone was now the leader of one of the largest and most powerful criminal organizations in the entire country. He was just twenty-six years old.

Prior to Torrio's death, however, Al Capone had been deeply involved in

restaurant. Some say the job was pulled off by Torrio and Capone's old Five Points pal, Frankie Yale. Whoever the trigger man was, though, Torrio was now in charge of Colosimo's empire, and Al Capone was promoted to Number Two man in the Chicago outfit.

During Prohibition, Chicago, much like New York, was divided by rival gangs, each vying for their own piece of the rumrunning action. One of those gangs, the North Siders, was headed by Irish mobster Dion O'Banion, who seemed to harbor a certain amount of personal animosity towards Torrio. One story tells of O'Banion selling a brewery to Torrio, knowing full well it was about to be raided by the cops, having probably tipped them off himself. The feud that followed escalated into a full-scale gang war that included many deaths on both sides, starting with O'Banion's.

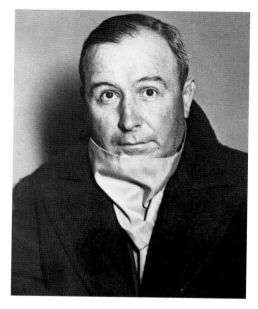

turning city politics in the gang's favor, using strong-arm tactics in the 1924 elections to ensure the success of the candidates whom he backed. Election Day in the Chicago suburb of Cicero, home to the gang's headquarters, was marked by violence and bloodshed, most notably with the death of Capone's older brother, Frank. Al Capone had sent out thugs to threaten, kidnap and even kill election officials, intimidate voters, and stuff ballot boxes. He would do anything to swing the elections in favor of his candidates. The day was quickly turning out to be a violent free-for-all, and police were dispatched to try to restore order. Working as an enforcer at the polls,

Frank Capone was gunned down by police when Frank, perhaps assuming the plain-clothed cops to be rival mobsters, drew his gun and started shooting. Al Capone's candidates ended up winning in a landslide, but he paid a great price for that victory, both personally and politically.

Meanwhile, the war between Capone and the North Siders continued. A second attempt on Capone's life was made on September 26, 1926, this time at his Cicero headquarters, the Hawthorne Inn. By some accounts, over 1,000 bullets were sprayed through the doors and windows of the hotel and adjoining restaurant. Capone, dining inside the

Above: Fashion plate Al Capone (right) with attorney Abe Tietelbaum in Florida, 1941.

opinion toward Al Capone and his barbaric methods. It happened on February 14, 1929, when seven members of the North Side Gang were savagely machine-gunned by Capone men dressed as cops.

The St. Valentine's Day Massacre essentially marked the beginning of the end for Al Capone. Law enforcement had been trying to hobble Capone for some time, but the massacre galvanized public opinion and steeled the government's resolve to bring down Capone one way or another. The attack was mounted on several fronts. An agent with the Prohibition Bureau, Eliot Ness, was charged with assembling a team of incorruptible men to find evidence of bootlegging and to generally harass Capone. Ness and his small band of agents, known as the Untouchables, have become legendary in their own right, immortalized in films and on a popular television series. Another team from the IRS was charged with building a case against Capone for income tax evasion. In 1927, the government estimated Al

Above: Actor Rod Steiger as "Scarface" in the 1959 film, Al Capone.

Opposite, top: Cubs catcher Gabby Harnett signing autograph for Al Capone and son, Al Jr., at Wrigley Field in 1931. Behind Capone is one of his bodyguards, reaching into his jacket, perhaps for his wallet so he can buy some popcorn.

restaurant, was again thrown to the floor by his bodyguard and again escaped unhurt. Miraculously, despite the quite literal scattergun approach to his attempted assassination, no one else was seriously injured, either.

Capone had enough of the North Siders and began taking out its leaders, each in turn. First was Hymie Weiss, machine-gunned outside of his headquarters in October of 1926. Next to fall was Vincent "the Schemer" Drucci in 1927, although he was shot by cops, apparently while handcuffed in the back seat of a squad car. After Drucci was gone, the leadership of the North Siders fell to George "Bugs" Moran. The plan to get the fearsome Moran was simple in its execution because that's exactly what it was—an execution. Although the operation missed its intended target, Moran, it did succeed in ending the North Side Gang. It also poisoned public

---

—— VITAL SIGNS ——

Born: January 17, 1899
Died: January 25, 1947
Cause of Death: Natural causes (heart failure)
Buried: Mount Carmel Cemetery; Hillside, Illinois

—— SCREEN TIME ——

Dillinger and Capone (1995). Played by F. Murray Abraham
The Untouchables (1987). Played by Robert DeNiro
Capone (1975). Played by Ben Gazzara
The St. Valentine's Day Massacre (1967). Played by Jason Robards
Al Capone (1959). Played by Rod Steiger

Capone to be worth $100 million, although through creative bookkeeping, Scarface was worth virtually nothing on paper.

In 1930, the Chicago Crime Commission put together a list of the city's top criminals, and Al Capone headed the list, with the dubious title of Public Enemy Number One (a precursor to the FBI's Ten Most Wanted list). Between his damaged public image, the harassment by Eliot Ness and the dogged pursuit of the IRS, Capone's days as a free man and mob boss were numbered. His trial for tax evasion found Capone bribing members of the jury only to have the judge switch the panel at the last moment. In its case, the prosecution employed a recent Supreme Court decision, aimed specifically at prosecuting mobsters, which ruled that income taxes had to be paid on all money made, regardless of whether the income was generated legally or illegally.

On October 17, 1931, Al Capone was found guilty of income tax evasion. He was sent off to the U.S. Penitentiary in 1932 where he reportedly lived a life of relative luxury. When authorities caught wind of his less-than-ascetic lifestyle, they shipped Capone off to the most infamous of prisons, Alcatraz, housing the worst of the worst in the middle of San Francisco Bay. Stripped of his influence and subjected to the harsh environment of the Rock, Capone spent his days slowly losing his mind to an untreated case of syphilis. He was finally released in November of 1939, and retired to his estate in Palm Island, Florida. There he lived out the remaining years of his life, gradually succumbing to the dementia brought on by his disease. He died of heart failure on January 25, 1947. Although he was only the head of the Chicago Outfit for about six years, his legacy lives on. The name Al "Scarface" Capone will forever be synonymous with the era of Prohibition in the roaring '20s, and the golden age of the mob.

Above: The Rock: Al Capone arrived at Alcatraz on August 22, 1934. It would be his home for the next five years.

Murder and Mayhem

In his time, Capone was said to be responsible for some 500 murders, either directly or indirectly. The figure may be much inflated, but there are ample stories illustrating his lust for blood. Not the least of which is a tale which describes Al inviting some double crossing mobsters, John Scalise and Albert Anselmi, over for dinner, after which he beat them each to death with a baseball bat at the table where they had all just dined. Another story tells of Capone having his old friend and mentor, Frankie Yale, gunned down in Brooklyn after learning that the New York mobster had been hijacking Al's booze shipments. Add to that the reported deaths from election intimidation, police cut down in the line of duty, and the many gang wars for control of Chicago, and the six-year reign of Al Capone marks one of the bloodiest periods in American history since the Civil War.

Heyday
Organized Crime After Repeal

February 8, 1932:
Vincent "Mad Dog"
Coll murdered

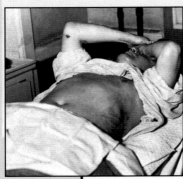

November 16, 1939:
Al Capone released
from prison

October 23, 1935:
Dutch Schultz shot,
dies the next day

June 12, 1941:
Harry "Pittsburgh
Phil" Strauss
executed

December 5, 1933:
Prohibition
repeal ratified

June 7, 1936:
Charles "Lucky"
Luciano sentenced
to 30-50 years

1932   1933   1934   1935   1936   1937   1938   1939   1940   19

January 25, 1947:
Al Capone
dies

February 9, 1946:
Lucky Luciano
deported to Italy

1950:
Kefauver Committee
hearings investigate
organized crime

March 4, 1944:
Louis "Lepke"
Buchalter executed
in Sing Sing
electric chair

June 20, 1947:
Bugsy Siegel murdered

| 42 | 1943 | 1944 | 1945 | 1946 | 1947 | 1948 | 1949 | 1950 |

Heyday
Organized Crime After Repeal

The end of the Castellammarese War essentially marked the birth of modern organized crime. Even before the end of Prohibition, the Syndicate had a defined structure for setting mob protocol, dividing territory, and enforcement. By the time Prohibition was repealed with the 21st Amendment, organized crime had already diversified into other areas of crime to ensure its own survival.

During the 1930s and '40s, the Syndicate enjoyed a continued period of relative peace and prosperity. Many mobsters made fortunes by taking control of the labor unions. Owning certain aspects of labor essential to daily business, like the trucking industry for instance, allowed mobsters the power to dictate operating fees, extort huge sums from management to avoid labor strikes, and the opportunity to skim union dues. Other mobsters expanded into narcotics trafficking, prostitution, even murder for hire. But the biggest money to be made in the post-Prohibition underworld was in gambling.

In the early 1950s, the Senate Special Committee to Investigate Crime in Interstate Commerce, led by Senator Estes Kefauver of Tennessee, began touring the United States, handing out subpoenas compelling many of the country's mobsters to testify, mainly on the subject of illegal gambling. The Kefauver Committee essentially marked the first time in U.S. history that organized crime was confronted on a national level. Many mobsters who had previously remained in the shadows were suddenly exposed to the limelight of national attention, facing the often dogged questioning of the Senate panel, before a rapt American audience who followed the televised hearings.

Despite the FBI's continued denials of the existence of organized crime, the Kefauver Committee hearings gave credibility to the notion of a highly organized national crime coalition. For many mobsters it was the end of business as usual.

Opposite: Former Prohibition enforcement agents, Izzy Einstein and Moe Smith, toasting the ratification of the 21st Amendment to the U.S. Constitution in 1933 which officially repealed Prohibition.

Left: Senator Estes Kefauver (seated) captivated America's attention in the early 1950s with televised hearings that delved into the nation's illegal gambling industry. Many of the biggest mobsters of the day were called to testify. It was quite a show.

Pittsburgh Phil

"He was vicious as a Gestapo agent, as casually cold-blooded as a meat-grinding machine in a butcher shop. He has such a lust for bloodletting that he would volunteer to handle 'contracts' even when it was not his turn to work."
—PROSECUTOR BURTON B. TURKUS
DESCRIBING HARRY STRAUSS IN HIS BOOK *Murder, Inc.*

Harry "Pittsburgh Phil" Strauss was thirty-three years old when he was put to death in New York's electric chair on June 12, 1941. He was executed for having committed murder. By many accounts, he could have been executed for the same crime over a hundred times. Pittsburgh Phil, a premier member of Murder, Inc., was one of the mob's most prolific killers.

Growing up in the Brownsville section of Brooklyn during the early part of the twentieth century was no picnic. It was on those mean streets that Harry Strauss learned his trade as a killer. It was also there that Pittsburgh Phil, as he was called for reasons unknown, met and teamed up with a group of friends and associates who would later become the deadly enforcement arm of the national crime Syndicate. They met, ironically, at Midnight Rose's candy store at the corner of Livonia and Saratoga Avenues. With killers like Happy Maione, Buggsy Goldstein, Frank Abbandando, Mendy Weiss, Abe Reles, and Pittsburgh Phil himself, Murder, Inc., reportedly carried out hundreds (some contend up to 1,000) mob hits across the country.

When dealing with shady figures like Pittsburgh Phil, the facts are often distorted, twisted, and, at the very least, exaggerated. But in 1940, district attorneys across the country had evidence linking Phil to nearly sixty murders. It is likely that Pittsburgh Phil was responsible for many more murders where there was no evidence. How many more will never be known.

There are several stories about Phil's deadly exploits, however. One important

Opposite: New York Police Department mug shot of Harry "Pittsburgh Phil" Strauss in 1940.

Left: Harry Strauss (right) and Martin "Buggsy" Goldstein (center) are arraigned in New York on April 12, 1940, for the murder of Puggy Feinstein. Both men would die in the electric chair for the crime. Seen at left is prosecutor Burton B. Turkus.

Right: The men of Murder, Inc., in a police lineup. (Left to right) Strauss, Harry "Happy" Maione, Frank "The Dasher" Abbandando. Maione and Abbandando also died in the electric chair, convicted of the brutal murder of loan shark Whitey Rudnick.

tale, from testimony by murderer-turned-stoolie, Abe "Kid Twist" Reles, describes a contract hit on one Irv "Puggy" Feinstein that Phil and Buggsy Goldstein committed in Rele's own living room while his elderly mother-in-law was asleep in the next room. They reportedly woke the woman up to ask where the rope and ice pick were kept. The hit was ordered by Albert Anastasia, The Lord High Executioner, himself, to

— VITAL SIGNS —

Born: July 28, 1909
Died: June 12, 1941
Cause of Death: Executed (electrocution)
Buried: Beth David Cemetery; Elmont, New York

put a stop to Puggy's running his one-man gambling operation that might bleed mob income. Anastasia ordered a "clean" hit, meaning no body should be found. A technique was used to tie the victim in such a way that his struggling would tighten the rope around his neck, slowly strangling himself to death. Goldstein then drove the body to a vacant lot and set it afire.

Another story tells of a body surfacing in Loch Sheldrake lake in the Catskill Mountains, after having been stabbed nearly thirty-six times and tied to a pinball machine. Pittsburgh Phil, on hearing of the reappearance of the body that he thought he had made sure would not be found, was said to reply, "With this bum, you gotta be a doctor or he floats."

Phil's career as mob hitman came to an end in 1940 when Abe Reles turned stool pigeon to save his own skin, and in the process brought down the whole of Murder, Inc. It was the Puggy Feinstein murder that Reles described to the D.A. that proved Phil's undoing. At his trial, Pittsburgh Phil offered little defense, but rather acted as though he'd gone insane, even chewing on his lawyer's brief case. He kept the act up even on death row, hoping for a reprieve. It never came. Phil finally dropped his act when he realized that nothing and no one could save him. He offered to turn states evidence if he could have a moment alone with the man who had ratted him out, Kid Twist Reles. The authorities wisely rejected Strauss's offer. By the time Reles was done spilling his guts, New York's electric chair would end the lives of Murder, Inc., career killers Mendy Weiss, Buggsy Goldstein, Happy Maione, Frank Abbandando, Louis Lepke, and Pittsburgh Phil himself.

Frank Costello reportedly paid $100,000 to have Kid Twist Reles thrown out a Coney Island hotel window while in police custody, otherwise he may have

helped put a few more mobsters in the chair. But it was too late for Harry "Pittsburgh Phil" Strauss. New York State worked quickly in those days. At 11:03 P.M. on June 12, 1941, Buggsy Goldstein died in the electric chair. At 11:06 P.M., Harry "Pittsburgh Phil" Strauss followed suit.

Above: Abe "Kid Twist" Reles in custody. His testimony led to the execution of several members of Murder, Inc., including Louis "Lepke" Buchalter.

Left: The body of Kid Twist Reles viewed from the Coney Island hotel window from which he fell to his death. Obviously this stool pigeon couldn't fly.

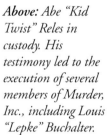

Dutch Schultz

"Come on, Max, open the soap duckets. Frankie, please come here. Open that door, Dumpey's door. It is so much, Abe, that…with the brewery. Come on. Hey, Jimmie! The chimney sweeps. Talk to the sword. Shut up, you got a big mouth! Please come help me up, Henny. Max come over here…French Canadian bean soup… I want to pay, let them leave me alone…"

—Dutch Schultz's feverish last words as transcribed

by a police stenographer from Schultz's deathbed

When people think of mobsters, one of the first names that comes to mind is Dutch Schultz. The image the name conjures is of a tough, ruthless and powerful mobster. The Beer Baron of the Bronx. This was an unpredictable, dangerous man to be reckoned with. Arthur Flegenheimer knew his given name would inspire no such awe or fear. That's why he changed his name to Dutch Schultz.

Arthur Simon Flegenheimer was born in the Bronx, New York, on August 6, 1902, the son of German-Jewish parents. In Arthur's early teens, his father walked out on the family, and the young man soon began running with a dangerous crowd. His mentor was a local street hood who enlisted the young Flegenheimer as muscle for his petty rackets. It wasn't long before Arthur was arrested and sent to jail, serving fifteen months on burglary charges, as well as time added for a failed prison escape attempt. It was at this time that Arthur Flegenheimer, perhaps wanting a name that fit his lifestyle, acquired the name Dutch Schultz. It had a nice ring to it.

When Dutch Schultz emerged from prison, Prohibition had recently become U.S. law, and bootleggers everywhere were cashing in. Schultz began working as a rumrunner in an operation connected with mobster, gambler, and underworld mentor, Arnold Rothstein.

Opposite: Arthur Flegenheimer, aka Dutch Schultz, in court in Albany, New York, 1934. Schultz was released on $75,000 bail while awaiting trial for income tax evasion.

Left: A worried looking Dutch Schultz awaits the verdict in his trial for tax evasion in Malone, New York, on August 1, 1935.

Right: The Beer Baron of the Bronx smokes a cigarette in the Manhattan federal courthouse in 1935.

Many of Schultz's generation of mobsters grew under the tutelage of Rothstein, and like his contemporaries, it wasn't long before Schultz decided to open up shop for himself. His territory was his own stomping grounds, one of New York City's five boroughs, the Bronx. Schultz partnered with a friend, Joey Noe, at first owning and operating speakeasies, before expanding into the manufacture and distribution of beer. This included forcing out the competition, as well as "persuading" speakeasy owners to buy their product. Bootlegging was certainly lucrative, but it was in the numbers rackets where the Dutchman made his real money.

The numbers racket, also known as policy, was enormously popular, especially in poor communities where the pennies and nickels wagered might bring a small payoff to the winner, and millions per year for the policy bankers. Similar to a lottery, bettors would give a small amount, perhaps only a penny, for a set of numbers. The winning numbers

were chosen based on horse races from tracks around the country. One of the richest areas for policy bankers was Harlem, a heavily black neighborhood in upper Manhattan. Dutch Schultz saw how much money there was to be made and he decided he wanted in on it. He had little trouble muscling into the policy bankers of Harlem, with the exception of Stephanie St. Clair, the "Policy Queen of Harlem." St. Clair tried to wage war against Schultz, but eventually succumbed to the wealth and power of the politically connected Dutchman.

Dutch Schultz was not well liked. With his taste for power and wealth combined with a disinclination to play nice with others, he often stepped on the toes of fellow mobsters. Jack "Legs" Diamond was one such mobster. A war broke out between the two when Schultz began expanding into Legs' area of Manhattan. The war would take the lives of many men on both sides, including Joey Noe and eventually Diamond himself, who was killed by suspected Schultz gunmen in 1931. Another war was with Vincent "Mad Dog" Coll. Casualties of that war included a five-year-old boy, accidentally killed in the crossfire as Coll was gunning for one of Schultz's men, Joey Rao. Coll, too, was a victim of the war, getting his in a phone booth with a Tommy gun wielded by gunmen possibly connected to Schultz.

The law, too, declared war on Dutch Schultz, and fared about as well as Coll and Diamond. A charge that would be used to bring down many mobsters, tax evasion, was brought out against Dutch Schultz, who was raking in millions on policy rackets alone. The first trial in upstate New York brought a hung jury. The second trial brought acquittal.

Schultz's defense was that he had offered the government money for back taxes, some $100,000, but the IRS refused to take it, saying Schultz owed far more. As weak as the defense was, the jury for some reason bought it (some say it was the jury who was bought) and Schultz walked away a free man.

But mobsters rarely beat the tax rap. While Schultz was upstate battling the government, his underboss, Abe "Bo" Weinberg, betting that his boss would be convicted, rolled the dice and handed over Schultz's empire to Lucky Luciano, whose recently formed national crime Syndicate immediately began parceling out the Dutchman's assets and territory to various Syndicate members. It was a bad bet for Weinberg. When Schultz

Below: August 2, 1935: A relieved Dutch Schultz leaves the Malone, New York, courthouse where a "not guilty" verdict was delivered on charges of tax evasion. Schultz arrived in the town well before his trial began in order to build good will among the people of Malone. The tactic seems to have worked.

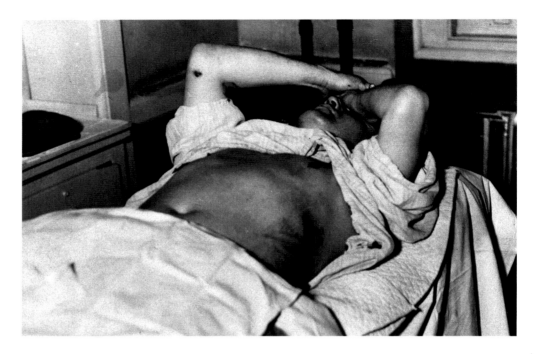

Right: Schultz on his deathbed, October 23, 1935, where he delivered his cryptic, feverish last words.

Below: Inside the Palace Chop House where the Dutchman was shot along with three others.

Opposite, bottom: A crowd gathers outside the Palace Chop House in Newark, New Jersey, where Dutch Schultz and three of his men were shot. Charles "the Bug" Workman served twenty-five years for the murders.

Opposite, top: There's gold in them thar hills. The Catskill Mountains in upstate New York.

returned to the city and found his empire had been divvied up by the mob, he went looking for blood, Weinberg's blood. One story has Dutch Schultz finding Weinberg exiting New Jersey mobster Waxey Gordon's mansion, and killing the traitor with his bare hands. Another has Weinberg taking a swim in one of New York's waterways while wearing concrete overshoes. Either way, Weinberg was never seen again. And Dutch Schultz was looking to regain his empire.

Thomas E. Dewey was a thorn in the mob's side, and Dutch Schultz's in particular. In 1934, Dewey, a special prosecutor for New York, was after the Dutchman, and Schultz, in turn, decided to go after the prosecutor. Breaking away from mob code that called those outside the mob off limits, Schultz approached

---

— VITAL SIGNS —

Born: August 6, 1902
Died: October 24, 1935
Cause of Death: Murdered (shot)
Buried: Gate of Heaven Cemetery; Hawthorne, New York

— SCREEN TIME —

Hoodlum (1997). Played by Tim Roth
Billy Bathgate (1991). Played by Dustin Hoffman
Portrait of a Mobster (1961). Played by Vic Morrow

---

the Syndicate, asking that Dewey be killed. The Syndicate ruling body, known as the Commission, comprised of the heads of the various crime families in the region, balked at Schultz's proposal. Schultz vowed to take matters into his own hands, promising to kill Dewey with or without the Commission's blessing. The Commission, fearing the repercussions of murdering a prominent court officer, decided that the Dutchman had to go.

The Palace Chop House in Newark, New Jersey, was the scene of the hit. In the line of fire were three of Schultz's men, Bernard "Lulu" Rosencrantz, Abe "Misfit" Landau, and Otto "Abbadabba" Berman, all shot down in the restaurant, along with Schultz himself. The hitmen were Charles "The Bug" Workman, and Emmanuel "Mendy" Weiss, two of the Syndicate's best assassins. Rosencrantz, Landau, and Berman all died on the spot but the Dutchman lived for a time and was taken to Newark Hospital, mortally wounded and delirious.

In his fevered delirium, Dutch Schultz faded in and out of consciousness. In his moments of wakefulness, Schultz spewed forth a rambling and cryptic diatribe on everything and nothing. Detectives tried to question Schultz on who had shot him, a police stenographer recording every word. The transcription of Dutch Schultz's deathbed words, at times haunting and poetic, has gone on to inspire writings such as William S. Burrough's *The Last Words of Dutch Schultz*, as well as being the focus of study for literary scholars and even college courses.

A telegram arrived at Newark Hospital for Dutch Schultz. It was from Stephanie St. Clair, the former Policy Queen of Harlem whom the Dutchman had forced out of business so many years before. It read, "As ye sow, so shall ye reap." Dutch Schultz died on October 24, 1935, never revealing the identity of his murderers. He was buried under a tombstone bearing the name Arthur Flegenheimer.

Mob Treasure Hunt

Just like stories of hidden pirates' treasure, there are many stories about hidden mobsters' treasures—from the ill-advised, live-televised opening of Al Capone's secret vault by Geraldo Rivera, to stories of Dutch Schultz's fortune buried in the Catskill Mountains. The tale goes that Schultz, thinking he was going to be sent to prison for tax evasion, wanted some scratch to return to after his sentence was over, so he stashed a bundle of cash somewhere in upstate New York. Some of the Dutchman's cryptic deathbed ramblings fueled the speculation, with a reference to the woods near Phoenecia, New York. The search continues today, with entire books having been written on the subject and even television mystery shows have taken up the investigation.

F. B. I. - N. Y.
LOUIS BUCHALTER
0-302-N2660
AUG 23 1939

Louis "Lepke" Buchalter

"All I want to say is I'm innocent. I'm here on a framed-up case. Give my love to my family and everything."

—LAST WORDS OF LOUIS BUCHALTER BEFORE HIS EXECUTION

The only mob boss ever to be executed by the state. Think about that for a minute. In the entire history of the organized crime in America, only one man who was in a position to be considered the head of a major crime family was ever executed. Through all the many decades, all the billions of dollars bilked from the American public, through mob stoolies and government informants, wiretaps and surveillance, through Senate hearings and vast political corruption, and through thousands of mob murders and assassinations, only one organized crime boss was ever convicted according to the laws of the United States and put to death. Whether it's an indictment of the American judicial system, or a testament to the enforced silence among mobsters, Louis "Lepke" Buchalter is the holder of that dubious title.

One of the few early mobsters who was a native of the United States, Louis Buchalter was born in New York City on February 6, 1897. His nickname, "*Lepke*," is a form of a Yiddish word meaning "little one," usually a term of endearment. His early entry into the world of crime was in the labor rackets, which would remain one of his main enterprises. He served as muscle under the tutelage of Jacob "Little Augie" Orgen, who also dabbled in bootlegging. Among Lepke's contemporaries in the gang were Jack "Legs" Diamond and Jacob "Gurrah" Shapiro, a no-necked Jewish thug with an accented growl of a voice that made "get out of here" sound like "Gurrah here!" Hence the nickname. Orgen's particular labor racket was mainly the low-finesse, barbaric game of strike-breaking, also called slugging. Orgen would use his thugs to do the bidding of whichever side of a labor dispute would pay more, sometimes playing both ends, taking money from both strikers and management at the same time.

Like many of the up-and-coming young mobsters of the day, Buchalter came to find an underworld mentor in Arnold Rothstein. A gambler, rackets financer, and elder statesmen of organized crime, Rothstein counseled Buchalter to urge Orgen to update his labor rackets. Orgen's methods were considered outmoded and were drawing increasing police scrutiny. The better method of controlling the labor rackets was to take over the labor unions, then extort money from management in exchange for avoided strikes, and maintain peace and profits for all. Besides

Opposite: 1939 mug shot of Louis Lepke following his surrender to the FBI's J. Edgar Hoover. It is believed that Lepke was tricked into surrendering by fellow mobsters.

Left: Lepke, guarded by an agent with a machine gun, arrives in court on July 20, 1943, where he was to receive the death sentence.

$5,000 REWARD

On November 8, 1937, Homer Cummings, Attorney General of the United States, under authority vested in him by law, offered the following rewards:

$2,500 for information furnished to the Federal Bureau of Investigation resulting in the apprehension of **JACOB SHAPIRO;**

$2,500 for information furnished to the Federal Bureau of Investigation resulting in the apprehension of **LOUIS BUCHALTER.**

The photographs and descriptions of the above named persons are hereinafter set out.

Jacob Shapiro was convicted in Federal Court at New York, New York, on November 8, 1936, of violating the Federal Antitrust Laws, and was sentenced to serve two years in a Federal penitentiary and to pay $10,000 fine. On appeal, this conviction was affirmed, and on June 14, 1937, upon his failure to surrender to the United States Marshal, as ordered, his bail in the amount of $10,000 was declared forfeit and a warrant issued for his arrest.

An indictment was returned by the Federal Grand Jury at New York, New York, on November 6, 1933, charging Shapiro and Buchalter, and others, with violating the Federal Antitrust Laws. Both Shapiro and Buchalter failed to appear in Federal Court for trial on July 6, 1937, and bail in the amount of $5,000 for each was forfeited and warrants issued for their arrests on July 7, 1937.

No part of the aforesaid rewards shall be paid to any officials or employees of the Department of Justice. The right is reserved to divide and allocate portions of any of said rewards as between several claimants. The offer provides that all claims to any of the above described rewards and all questions and disputes that may arise as among claimants to the foregoing rewards shall be passed upon by the Attorney General and that his decisions shall be final and conclusive.

Photographs taken February 16, 1936.

Photographs taken June 12, 1933.

JACOB SHAPIRO, with aliases: "GURRAH," CHARLES SHAPIRO, MORRIS FRIEDMAN, SAMUEL DISHOUSE, SAMUEL DISNAHUSEN.

DESCRIPTION: Age, 41 or 42 years (born in Russia about 1895); height, 5' 5½"; weight, 200 lbs.; build, stocky; nationality, Russian, Jewish; hair, medium chestnut; eyes, blue, wears glasses occasionally; complexion, medium - inclined to be flushed; features, large mouth, thick lips, nose somewhat flattened - appearance of having been broken (possibly remodeled by plastic surgery) - large ears; dress, rather conservative - well tailored; speech, very guttural, Jewish accent; mannerisms, gesticulates with hands when speaking; peculiarities, thick hands and short stubby fingers; fingerprint classification, 11 11 R O 7 Ref: 9, 3, 1 / 26 R 1 / 26 26 26

LOUIS BUCHALTER, with aliases: "LEPKE," LOUIS BUCKHOUSE, LOUIS BUCKHALTER, LOUIS KAWER, LOUIS COHEN, LOUIS BUCKALTER.

DESCRIPTION: Age, 40 years (born February 12, 1897, at New York City); race, white - Jewish; height, 5' 5½"; weight, 160 lbs.; build, medium; hair, dark brown or black; eyes, brown; complexion, dark; peculiarities, nose - large, rather straight and blunt - ears - prominent - eyes - alert and shifting; marital status, married - one son, Harold, aged about 17; fingerprint classification, 25 11 17. / 27 O

Information may be communicated in person, or by telephone or telegraph collect, to the undersigned, or to the nearest office of the Federal Bureau of Investigation, United States Department of Justice, the local addresses and telephone numbers of which are set forth on the reverse side of this notice.

JOHN EDGAR HOOVER, DIRECTOR,
FEDERAL BUREAU OF INVESTIGATION,
UNITED STATES DEPARTMENT OF JUSTICE,
WASHINGTON, D. C.
TELEPHONE, NATIONAL 7117.

November 8, 1937.

Above: 1937 Wanted Poster issued for the capture of Louis Buchalter and Jacob "Gurrah" Shapiro.

that, union dues could be manipulated and coffers skimmed.

However, Little Augie, like his Sicilian contemporaries Giuseppe Masseria and Salvatore Maranzano, was set in his old ways and wouldn't budge. Louis Lepke saw no other option than to do away with the old and usher in the new. In 1927, Buchalter and Gurrah Shapiro ambushed Orgen and shot him down in the street, killing him and injuring Legs Diamond. Buchalter and Shapiro procured Orgen's labor rackets and, perhaps to avoid hard feelings, gave the bootlegging to Legs Diamond.

Louis Lepke and Gurrah Shapiro next turned their sights on the garment indus-

try. Using their experience in the labor rackets, the two mobsters set about infiltrating the New York clothing industry, and through a combination of cunning and intimidation, Lepke and Shapiro were soon able to leverage themselves into ownership positions in several garment businesses. Taking a page from Little Augie's playbook, anyone who resisted was fiercely beaten or killed. Next, the duo moved into the baking industry by controlling flour trucking.

With the power gained from his rackets, Louis Buchalter was asked to join the national crime Syndicate that was being formed after the resolution of the Castellammarese War. Perhaps it was Lepke's fearsome reputation or his businesslike willingness to kill when necessary; Buchalter was asked to run the enforcement arm of the Syndicate. The group would act on the orders of the ruling board, known as the Commission, keeping peace in the Syndicate by any means necessary, dispensing justice, punishing the wayward, and silencing any witnesses brave or stupid enough to testify against them. The group would also serve to deter anyone who thought of breaking the code of silence, thus ensuring protection from legal prosecution. Buchalter accepted the position and young killers were recruited for the new group. Much later, a crime reporter for the New York *World Telegram* would famously dub the group "Murder, Inc."

Sharing in the administration of Murder, Inc. was Albert Anastasia, who had a murderous reputation in his own right. Among the professional killers in the group were such notorious names as Happy Maione, Harry "Pittsburgh Phil" Strauss, Mendy Weiss, Charles "the Bug" Workman and Abe "Kid Twist" Reles. Murder, Inc., did not merely serve to enforce, but also to intimidate. As such, their methods of murder were often purposely sadistic and gruesome in order to serve as warnings to those who might cross the Syndicate. Depending on the nature of the infraction, the condemned might die with a quick, painless bullet in the back of the head, or in a very

VITAL SIGNS

Born: February 6, 1897
Died: March 4, 1944
Cause of Death: Executed (electrocution)
Buried: Mount Hebron Cemetery; Queens, New York

SCREEN TIME

Lepke (1975). Played by Tony Curtis
Murder, Inc. (1960). Played by David J. Stewart

public hail of bullets on a street corner, or stabbed to death with an ice pick, or even buried alive. Bodies might be carved up, or stuffed in the trunk of a car, or often just disappear, never to be seen again. In short, while the techniques varied, there was a definite method to the madness.

Ironically, despite its charter to enforce the rules of the Syndicate, including the all-important code of silence, it was one of the killers of Murder, Inc., who ultimately brought down the organization and many of its members, including Louis Buchalter. The arrests of a number of fellow associates who were familiar with his work convinced Abe "Kid Twist" Reles that his own arrest was imminent. He weighed his options and decided that his choices were three: go on the lam until things blew over, take his chances with the law and possibly face the death penalty, or cut a deal to sing like Caruso in an effort to avoid the chair. Improbably, Reles chose the third option.

Meanwhile, the tenacious New York special prosecutor, Thomas E. Dewey, set his sights on Louis "Lepke" Buchalter, slapping him with labor extortion charges. Competing federal authorities each wanted a piece of Lepke as well. The ambient heat generated for the Syndicate provoked the decision that Buchalter had to turn himself in and face the music. One story tells of Lepke being misled by the Commission to believe that a deal had been struck in which he could turn himself in to the FBI and serve just five years on a narcotics charge. On August 24, 1939, the pre-arranged meeting place found Buchalter turning himself in to none other than FBI director J. Edgar Hoover himself, accompanied by his good friend, gossip columnist Walter Winchell. Louis Lepke soon found that there was no such deal. He'd been set up and was open to any and all prosecution.

Sitting in prison with a fourteen-year sentence for narcotics trafficking, in addition to another thirty-nine years piled on for the extortion rap, Lepke learned that Kid Twist had flipped. Reles fingered Buchalter in the 1936 murder of a candy store owner. The charges stuck and Lepke soon found himself sitting on death row.

For his part, Abe Reles went out a sixth floor window of a Coney Island, Brooklyn hotel while in protective police custody. It's not certain whether or not he had help. It mattered not for Louis Buchalter. Despite speculation in the media that he might flip to gain a stay of execution from now Governor Thomas E. Dewey, Louis Buchalter was put to death in New York's electric chair on March 4, 1944. Some say that he was the wealthiest man ever executed in the United States—yet another dubious honor for Louis Lepke.

Left: Lepke, with a cigar in his free hand, enters a New York paddy wagon in 1936.

Bugsy Siegel

"When we were in a fight Benny would never hesitate. He was even quicker to take action than those hot-blooded Sicilians, the first to start punching and shooting. Nobody reacted faster than Benny."
—MEYER LANSKY

In 1946, the Federal Bureau of Investigation's description of Benjamin "Bugsy" Siegel read as follows: "42 years, 5'9", 157 pounds; dark brown hair, grey-green eyes; medium complexion, medium build; Jewish." A bland and antiseptic description, to be sure (and in 1946 he was, in fact, forty years old). But there are many other things about Siegel that the thousands of pages contained in his FBI file leave out. Like the fact that, to many, Bugsy Siegel was the very embodiment of the mythologized mobster—handsome, suave, and deadly.

Benjamin Siegel was born on February 28, 1906, in Williamsburg, Brooklyn. The son of Russian-Jewish immigrants, Siegel was determined to rise above the poverty of the New York tenements. As a boy, Benny set up a protection racket where, for a price, he and his young associates would ensure that no harm would come to local street vendors. Any vendor who did not feel that protection was needed, especially protection provided by children, had their carts doused with kerosene and set ablaze. The protection money was soon forthcoming. The young hoodlum was quick to realize the value of violence in getting what he wanted. It was a lesson that would guide him throughout his life.

As a teenager, Siegel met and soon teamed up with another fellow Jewish hood, Meyer Lansky. There are several different versions of how the two outlaws met, but however it happened, the duo would go on to help create one of the most successful and deadly organized crime networks in the country. Lansky and Siegel were in many ways opposites. Lansky was cool and calculating, with a head for business. Siegel was emotion and action with a penchant for violence. With the combination of business sense and muscle the two formed what was to be known as the Bug and Meyer Mob. The boys built a reputation as an efficient murder-for-hire gang, predating and perhaps later used as a template for the Syndicate's enforcement arm, Murder, Inc.

Opposite: A dapper Benjamin Siegel in court on October 12, 1941, facing charges in the murder of Harry "Big Greenie" Greenberg.

Left: 1928 New York Police Department mug shot of Bugsy Siegel. The accompanying description lists his occupation as the owner of an insurance company.

But Lansky had bigger ideas for the Bug and Meyer Mob than just being hired guns. Expanding into rumrunning and hijacking during Prohibition, Lansky set about building a business relationship with contemporary Charles "Lucky" Luciano. Charlie Lucky was an ambitious and similarly-minded Sicilian mobster who had designs on taking over the mob from the old-time Mustache Petes and forming a nationwide crime syndicate that overlooked the old barriers of territory and ethnicity for the greater good of the bottom line. The two old-timers standing in their way were Luciano's boss, Giuseppe "Joe the Boss" Masseria, and Masseria's enemy and rival for control of the mob, Salvatore Maranzano. One of the quickest ways to get a promotion in the underworld is to hasten the retirement of those above you. Bugsy Siegel was reportedly one of the men who entered Gerardo Scarpato's Nuova Villa Tamarro restaurant in Coney Island, on April 15, 1931, and shot Masseria to death. Some reports also contend that Siegel was part of the hit squad of four Jewish guns to shoot and stab Maranzano to death in his office in midtown Manhattan four months after Masseria was forcibly retired. Whoever the actual triggermen were, the murders removed the last barriers to the forming of an organized crime syndicate that would help shape America.

As part of the new crime Syndicate, formed just prior to the repeal of Prohibition, the old Bug and Meyer Mob expanded into many new areas of illegal opportunity. The gang reportedly had hands in numbers rackets and drug trafficking, and also moved in to exploit both legal and illegal gambling and the race wire services across the country. In 1937, Lansky sent Benny Siegel to California to take over and expand the Syndicate's interests in western states. It was in California that Siegel came into his own and built the image that his name still conjures today.

Hollywood loves a good story and a pretty face and Bugsy Siegel fit the bill in spades. With matinee idol good looks, the charm of a leading man, and more edge than any Hollywood heavy, Bugsy was a perfect fit in Tinseltown. He was old friends with actor George Raft, who made his name playing mobsters on the big screen. The pair were a sight to see, with onlookers hard pressed to tell the real mobster from the fictional. Raft was even present when Siegel was arrested for racketeering, which led to his only felony conviction, despite a lifetime of murder and mayhem. This was a point of considerable pride with Bugsy. He got off with a $250 fine.

Siegel was also a hit with the ladies. Despite having a wife and two daughters, Benny was romantically linked to numerous socialites and starlets, including Countess Dorothy di Frasso and Jean Harlow, as well as a long and torrid affair with mob moll Virginia Hill. It was in Hill's mansion in Beverly Hills that Siegel would eventually meet his demise. But before that came Sin City.

Bugsy Siegel didn't discover Las Vegas, as many would have it. But he did help to build the image of wealth and glitz

Left: Glamour shot of mob moll and sometime actress, Virginia Hill.

that it has today. In the 1930s and '40s the mob was looking to exploit legal gambling wherever it could be found. In places like the Bahamas, Cuba and Nevada, mob-owned casinos were springing up, making enormous profits from

Left: Siegel (center) is congratulated by his defense attorneys, Byron Hanna (left) and Jerry Giesler after his indictment for the murder of Harry Greenberg was dropped by Los Angeles District Attorney John F. Dockweiler for lack of evidence on December 11, 1940.

The Flamingo

Virginia Hill was called to testify before the Kefauver Committee on April 6, 1951. Having had relationships with several mobsters, including Bugsy Siegel, Joe Adonis, and Chicago bookmaker, Joseph Epstein, Hill was of particular interest to the committee. Her testimony did not reveal anything of legal use to the senators, but she did put on quite a show. She reportedly punched a female reporter in the face following her testimony and publicly expressed her hopes that the members of the press would meet their ends with an atom bomb. During her testimony she was asked by one of the more prurient senators why she was so popular among mobsters. Hill attempted to deflect the question, but after being pressed, she responded that she was particularly good in bed, although her choice of words was a bit more heady in tone.

Above: Virginia Hill testifies before the Senate Special Committee to Investigate Crime in Interstate Commerce, also known as the Kefauver Committee, after its chairman, Senator Estes Kefauver.

pre-tax skimming. It's unclear whose idea it was to set up shop in the Nevada desert, but where there was big money to be made, the mob soon followed. With Syndicate funds, Bugsy began proffering the mob's race wire service, and building what would become the first Hollywood-style resort hotel-casino in Las Vegas, the Flamingo.

Dubbed for the nickname of his long-time mistress, Virginia Hill, the Flamingo was designed to be not merely a place to gamble, but a destination in itself. With fine food, lavish decoration, swimming pools, top-talent entertainment and a golf course in the works, Bugsy Siegel's pet project was an expensive proposition. The hotel cost some $6 million to build, well beyond original estimates, due in part to Bugsy's poor management. Contractors were apparently double-billing Benny, who was never much for bean counting. It is also suspected that Siegel was skimming construction money for himself and sending it off with Hill for deposit in European banks. Wherever the money was going, it was too much for the Syndicate. Bugsy was beginning to look like a liability that needed to be cut.

Cost overruns, political troubles, legal hurdles, and scheduling delays plagued Siegel and the Flamingo. The ill-timed grand opening on December 26, 1946, was less than spectacular. The Flamingo was closed for a time, then reopened in March of

Above: Los Angeles police photo of Bugsy Siegel, dead on the sofa of Virginia Hill's Beverly Hills mansion, June 20, 1947.

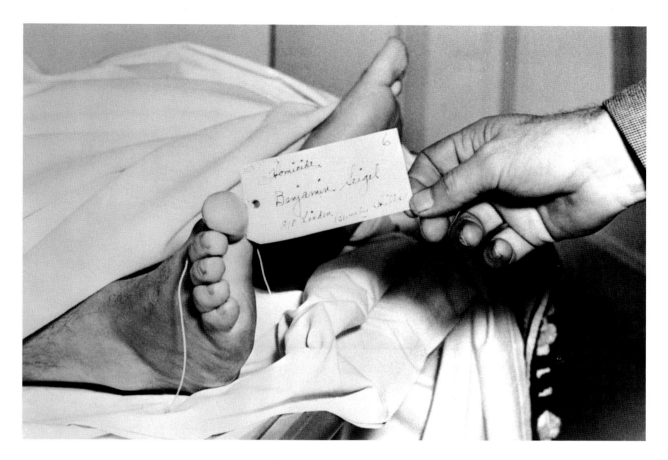

1947, and eventually began to show a return on the Syndicate's investment, although far below what was expected. It was clear that the problem was in the management office. The decision to make a change, as with all mob hits, came on a vote by the Syndicate's ruling body, the Commission. One of the members of the Commission was Meyer Lansky, who reluctantly signed off on his old friend's death warrant. Friendship was one thing, but business was business.

On June 20, 1947, Bugsy Siegel was relaxing on the sofa with a friend, Allen Smiley, when nine shots were fired from a rifle through the window of Virginia Hill's mansion. As an FBI report graphically described, "two bullets had entered Siegel's body through the head; one bullet came out through an eye, and a portion of an eyelid was found ten feet from him." Within hours of the shooting, Syndicate members walked into the Flamingo with news that the hotel was under new man-agement. Despite his seeming popularity in Hollywood, only five mourners attended the funeral. Pointedly, life-long friend Meyer Lansky wasn't one of them.

Above: As ye sow: Benjamin Siegel, identified by toe tag, in the Los Angeles County morgue.

——— **VITAL SIGNS** ———

Born: February 28, 1906
Died: June 20, 1947
Cause of Death: Murdered (shot)
Buried: Hollywood Forever Cemetery; Hollywood, California

——— **SCREEN TIME** ———

Bugsy (1991). Played by Warren Beatty
Mobsters (1991). Played by Richard Grieco
The Virginia Hill Story (1974) (TV). Played by Harvey Keitel (with Dyan Cannon as Virginia Hill)

Joe Adonis

"For looks, that guy's a bum."
—JOE ADONIS'S APPRAISAL OF RUDOLPH VALENTINO

In Greek mythology, Adonis was a youth whose striking beauty caused the goddess Venus to fall madly in love with him. The name still carries the image of an exceptionally handsome young man. It would take a big ego for someone to christen himself Adonis. One mobster did.

Giuseppe Doto was born in a small town near Naples, Italy, in 1902. Early records are hard to come by, as all his life Doto claimed to have been born in America. Various sources say that he arrived in the States around 1915, and soon, giving himself the name he felt he deserved, began calling himself Joe Adonis.

Adonis began his life in New York's underworld in Brooklyn, working for Frankie Yale, who had a successful bootlegging racket. Yale was aligned with Joe the Boss Masseria in the Castellammarese War against Salvatore Maranzano. With Yale's murder in 1928, Adonis took over much of the bootlegging in the Brooklyn territory. Somewhere along the line he met Lucky Luciano and Meyer Lansky and agreed with their philosophy that it was better for disparate gangs to work together for their own common good, than to have constant, counterproductive fighting over race and religion, and even fighting between Mafiosi from different regions of Italy. In order to restructure and organize, the old-fashioned Mustache Petes had to go, the first being Joe Masseria.

Four gunmen entered the Nuova Villa Tammaro restaurant in Coney Island on April 15, 1931, and gunned down Masseria. The gunmen are widely identified as Albert Ananstasia, Vito Genovese, Bugsy Siegel, and Joe Adonis. The next to go was Sal Maranzano, a mere four months after Masseria, shot and stabbed to death in his midtown Manhattan office by mobsters posing as cops. The new generation of mobsters took over and set about aligning gangs across the country with their newly emerging Syndicate.

One member of the Commission, the Syndicate's board of directors, was Joe Adonis. A story tells of a Commission meeting where Dutch Schultz, fed up with Adonis' ego, put the handsome mobster in a headlock and breathed a lungful of flu germs in his face. But despite his arrogance and reportedly "crippling" vanity, Adonis never sought to become *capo di tutti capi*, even though he probably had plenty of opportunity.

After Prohibition, Adonis, along with the Syndicate, expanded into a wide variety of moneymaking enterprises, investing heavily in gambling across the country, as well as numerous legitimate businesses. For instance, there was Joe's Italian Kitchen in Brooklyn, which Adonis naturally named for himself. When Luciano was sent to prison in 1936, he named Joe Adonis as the nominal head of the Syndicate, with help and support from Frank Costello and Meyer Lansky, although Luciano still had a significant voice from behind bars.

In 1944, Joe moved his headquarters from Brooklyn to New Jersey, and

Opposite: Joseph Doto, aka Joe Adonis, at police headquarters in Brooklyn, May 9, 1940.

Right Joe Adonis (standing at right) holds up his hand as he is sworn in by Senator Estes Kefauver (standing at left) before his testimony to the Senate committee investigating interstate crime. Adonis invoked his Fifth Amendment protection rights.

Below: Adonis (with hat) in Rome, Italy, on January 29, 1956, following his deportation from the United States. Adonis is flanked by Italian plain-clothed police, who regarded the mobster as a "socially undesirable element."

Commission meetings were said to be held in a secret back room of Duke's Restaurant in Cliffside Park, across the Hudson River from Manhattan. The heads of crime families and gangs from across the country would meet at Duke's to carry out the business of organized crime. Adonis also bought a trucking business in New Jersey, which aided other endeavors, from coin operated vending machines to the various water-front rackets. Through it all, Adonis managed to become very wealthy and, by greasing the right palms, out of the law's reach.

All that changed in 1950 when the Kefauver hearings came to town. Adonis was dragged in front of the television cameras for questioning, along with scores of other mobsters across the country, concerning his involvement in illegal gambling. The publicity that the hearings generated caused public offi-cials (who had been paid off to overlook mob matters) to head for the hills. Without his previous protection, on

May 28, 1951, Joe Adonis was convicted of illegal gambling activities and sent to prison for two years.

Upon his release in July of 1953, Justice Department investigators discovered that Joe Adonis was not an American citizen as

—— VITAL SIGNS ——

Born: November 22, 1902
Died: November 26, 1971
Cause of Death: Natural causes
Buried: Madonna Cemetery; Fort Lee, New Jersey

—— SCREEN TIME ——

Lansky (1999) (TV). Played by Sal Landi
Bugsy (1991). Played by Lewis Van Bergen

The Kennedy Clan

he had claimed before the Kefauver Committee. Adonis was ordered to return to his native Italy. The legal battle that followed lasted for nearly three years, finally ending only after Adonis agreed to leave the country voluntarily in exchange for a dropped perjury conviction that would have sent him back to prison and then deported anyway.

Joe Adonis settled in Milan, Italy. He had millions stashed away from his many decades as an American mobster, and lived a life of luxurious retirement. There are stories of a feud between Adonis and the similarly deported Luciano, most probably over a perceived lack of support on Adonis's part for Frank Costello's battles back in the States with Vito Genovese. Nevertheless, Adonis attended Luciano's funeral in Naples in 1962.

On November 26, 1971, Joe Adonis died of natural causes in Italy. The ex-mobster's body was returned to America, the land he always contended to be his place of birth. He was buried in Fort Lee, New Jersey, just across the George Washington Bridge from Manhattan.

Above: 1931 New York police mug shot of Adonis.

Above, right: (Left to right) President John F. Kennedy, FBI Director J. Edgar Hoover, Attorney General Robert F. Kennedy.

The alleged links between the mob and the Kennedy clan yield many intriguing stories. It is often rumored that Joseph P. Kennedy was engaged in bootlegging during Prohibition, although there is no direct evidence to that effect. Nevertheless, it is alleged that the Kennedys knew and associated with many mobsters, and that John F. Kennedy owed his election as president in 1960 to mob manipulation at the polls. But Kennedy's brother, Robert, had long had a reputation of pursuing organized crime, which only grew after he was appointed U.S. Attorney General. This dogged pursuit of organized criminals earned Bobby Kennedy no love among mobsters. One of the many unsubstantiated mob/Kennedy stories tells of the mob helping to elect JFK on the premise that Kennedy would help return Joe Adonis to America from his "exile" in Italy. But Bobby Kennedy put the kibosh on that plan. Regardless of the truthfulness of the story, Adonis stayed put.

Frank Costello

"Right now, I want to assure you of my loyalty for all you have done. It is unwavering."

—Judge Thomas A. Aurelio, as overheard in a wiretapped phone conversation with Frank Costello after Aurelio learned of his nomination to New York's Supreme Court

Like an aggressive dictator, Vito Genovese wanted to rule the mob in America. His technique was simple and time-tested: kill anyone who stood in his way. Namely, Albert Anastasia and Frank Costello. Anastasia was gunned down and killed in a barber chair in 1957, Costello was shot in the lobby of his Central Park West apartment building six months earlier. The way was clear now for Genovese to complete his domination of the underworld. The only problem was that Frank Costello, the "Prime Minister" of the mob, survived the attempt on his life.

A native of the Calabria region of Italy, Francesco Castiglia was born on January 20, 1891. He and his family arrived in New York in 1895, and by his teenaged years the young Francesco was running with street gangs. Before long, perhaps foreshadowing his proclivity for diplomacy, he became known as Frank Costello, a name appealing to both the Italians and the Irish with whom he associated. Mostly petty crime occupied Costello's time, exemplified by an eleven-month sentence he served in 1915 for carrying a gun. But like so many other street thugs of the early 20th century, Prohibition offered Costello the opportunity to move from small-time, petty rackets to a new era of unprecedented wealth. Those newfound riches in turn afforded him the opportunity to corrupt police and public officials and gain a measure of influence that had not previously been enjoyed.

Opposite: A contemptuous Frank Costello returns to testify before the Kefauver Committee on March 16, 1951, the day after he angrily walked out of the hearings.

Left: Costello gives money to a panhandler in New York, 1950.

Frank Costello was quick to realize that it was easier and more economical to buy influence and legal insulation than to fight the powers that be. This notion was particularly impressed upon him by underworld legend, Arnold Rothstein. Rothstein was a gambler who owned several illegal carpet (high-class gambling) joints, and who also financed many mobsters in their underworld endeavors. He also acted as a sort of mentor to an entire generation of mobsters who would soon usher in a new era of organized crime. Two other men, Charles "Lucky" Luciano and Meyer Lansky, would also be important, life-long allies of Costello's as the men set out to build a powerful coalition of gangs across the country that would comprise a national crime coalition.

Mostly into gambling rackets, Costello also held a position on the Syndicate's Commission as a sort of liaison between the underworld and the political establishment. Those Costello had in his pocket included many judges, prosecutors, police officials, and congressmen. One high-profile official who had an apparent "understanding" with

the world of organized crime was the director of the FBI, J. Edgar Hoover. For decades Hoover insisted that neither the Mafia nor organized crime even existed in the United States. However, there is evidence that Hoover may have been indirectly bought in exchange for his willful ignorance on the existence of the mob. Although there is no direct evidence that there was any formal agreement between Hoover and the Syndicate, it is clear that there was a system by which Hoover profited from their illegal activities.

The scheme was fairly simple. Hoover was an avid player of the ponies. The mob was deeply entrenched in horse racing, which included the fixing of races to make for sure bets. These sure things were passed from Costello to a close friend of Hoover's, newspaper columnist Walter Winchell, who in turn passed the tips on to Hoover himself. Although he did not publicly deny his enthusiasm for horse racing, Hoover did engage in a bit of sleight of hand when at the track. While the media witnessed Hoover's occasional trip to the $2 window to place a bet, an incognito FBI agent was dispatched to the high-stakes windows to act on the tips received from Winchell. Thus did Hoover profit from the illegal activities of the mob. Under Hoover, the FBI's official stance on the non-existence of organized crime in America lasted for over twenty-five years.

Despite his considerable influence, Frank Costello learned in the early 1950s that bought government officials were only good for so much. Once under the harsh glare of public scrutiny, it became every man for himself. The Kefauver Committee hearings were an abject lesson in this for Costello. Called to mostly examine illegal gambling in the United States, the televised committee hearings traveled across America questioning many criminals about their illegal activities, before finally setting up shop in New York, where many of the city's top mobsters were subpoenaed to testify. Costello was one of the star attractions. Two decisions that Costello made, which he supposed would help to convince both the committee and the country that

he was a legitimate businessman making an honest living, backfired and even helped to brand Costello as the top mobster in America.

The first of those decisions was the stipulation that Costello would appear before the committee only if the television cameras did not show his face, presumably so as not to taint his image as a reputable businessman. The cameras instead focused on Costello's hands, which lent an air of mystery to the man whose gravelly voice was the apparent model for Marlon Brando's Don Corleone in the film, *The Godfather*. The second decision Costello made was his angry walk out in the middle of the hearings, complaining of throat trouble. Combined with his many recitations of his Fifth Amendment rights, Costello was eventually given a short prison sentence for contempt of Congress.

Following the Kefauver hearings, Costello had several stays in prison, with jail time for tax evasion added to his contempt convictions. But it was a power struggle within the Syndicate that nearly

Left: Costello smokes as he testifies before the Kefauver Committee. Those who followed the hearings on television never saw Costello's face as cameras were instructed, at the insistence of his lawyers, to focus only on the mobster's hands.

Right: 1935 New York Police Department mug shot of Francesco Castiglia, aka Frank Costello.

Below: Costello, with a bandage on his head and blood on his coat, is escorted from Roosevelt Hospital by a police detective following an attempt on his life by Vincent "the Chin" Gigante in 1957.

Opposite, bottom: The "Prime Minister of the Underworld," Frank Costello (right) with his attorney George Wolf in 1943.

Opposite, top: Robert DeNiro (left) and Billy Crystal in the 1999 Warner Bros. release Analyze This.

proved Costello's end. Vito Genovese had his sights set on becoming the undisputed head of the underworld. After he returned from a self-imposed exile in Italy, Genovese set about building up his power base until, in 1957, he finally made his move. First, Genovese sought to take over the leadership of the family that Costello headed which had been inherited from the exiled Lucky Luciano. Shunning diplomacy, Genovese decided to have Costello killed. He chose Vincent "the Chin" Gigante as the hitman. On the evening of May 2, 1957, Costello was

waiting for an elevator in the lobby of his apartment building, when Gigante appeared and, perhaps having seen too many gangster movies, was heard to say, "This one's for you, Frank," before firing his pistol, hitting Costello in the head. Maybe more concerned about his dialogue than his aim, Gigante fled, assuming success. But the Chin's aim was not true. The bullet merely grazed the side of Costello's head. However, for a variety of reasons, not the least of which may have been to avoid a gang war, Costello officially retired as boss of the family.

--- **VITAL SIGNS** ---

Born: January 20, 1891
Died: February 18, 1973
Cause of Death: Natural causes (heart failure)
Buried: St. Michael's Cemetery; Queens, New York

--- **SCREEN TIME** ---

Bugsy (1991). Played by Carmine Caridi
Mobsters (1991). Played by Costas Mandylor

But Costello wouldn't go quietly. After Albert Anastasia's murder only five months after the attempt on Costello, Genovese called a meeting of Syndicate members from across the country, presumably to assume his role as *capo di tutti capi*. But a well-timed police raid at the site of the mob tête-à-tête in Apalachin, New York, brought an end to any such hopes for the gathering. There is speculation that someone with a bone to pick with Genovese may have tipped the cops off to the conference. It was the beginning of the end for Vito.

Genovese was finished off later that year when another tip, this time to the Feds, sent him off to prison on a fifteen-year narcotics conviction, where he eventually died. That frame job was the fruit of a collaboration between the exiled Luciano, Meyer Lansky, Carlo Gambino, and the Prime Minister of the underworld, Frank Costello. A few years later, Costello, serving time for contempt, was a resident of the same correctional facility as Genovese. The two reportedly had a reconciliation of sorts. Genovese *had* tried to kill him, but business is business, and no one understood that better than Costello.

Frank Costello retired from active involvement in the mob, passing into old age comfortably, living out his years on money made from a lifetime of crime. He died of heart failure on February 18, 1973, at the age of eighty-two.

Mob Mentality

Film and television have long enjoyed the idea of a tough mobster spending time on a psychiatrist's couch. The entertainment potential is self-evident. But it is well known that Frank Costello did actually consult a psychiatrist for two years.

From 1947 to 1949, Costello visited the offices of one Richard H. Hoffman, a Park Avenue psychiatrist known as the therapist to the rich and famous of New York City. Speculation is that Costello was having a bit of a mid-life crisis, suffering from anxiety and doubt over his chosen career.

When the press found out about the relationship, Hoffman admitted to reporters that he had been treating Costello, and that he had tried to introduce the mobster to a "better class of people." When Costello heard of this breach of confidence, he immediately broke off the relationship with the psychiatrist and informed the press that he had actually been the one to introduce Hoffman to a better class of people.

One notable film, *Analyze This (1999)*, starring Robert DeNiro and Billy Crystal, which comically explores the relationship between a mobster and his shrink, was a huge hit at the box office and spawned its sequel, *Analyze That* (2002). A similar relationship exists between Tony Soprano and Dr. Jennifer Melfi on HBO's *The Sopranos*.

Owney Madden

"Owney was really a guy to respect and admire—quite a guy, a man of his word. His faithfulness to his own kind is the strongest thing a man can have, and if Owney felt that you were an all right person, there wasn't nothing that he wouldn't do for you."
—MOBSTER MICKEY COHEN FROM HIS BOOK *In My Own Words*

One of the most famous speakeasies of the Prohibition era, the Cotton Club embodied the very spirit of the age of Jazz and the Roaring 20s. Some of the best and most famous black musicians and entertainers performed at the club, including Duke Ellington, Louis Armstrong, Cab Calloway, Bill "Bojangles" Robinson, Lena Horne, and the fast feet of the Nicholas Brothers. Fittingly, the most famous of gin joints was owned by a mobster: Owney Madden.

Born in Liverpool, England, in 1891 to Irish parents, Owen Madden was only nine years old when his father died. His mother, hoping to find a better life in America, moved the family to New York in 1903, and settled in the heavily Irish Manhattan neighborhood known as Hell's Kitchen. The young Owney soon began running with the young Irish hooligans that terrorized the area. Owney distinguished himself with his gift for brutality and soon earned himself the moniker "the Killer." He reportedly committed his first murder as a sort of celebration after winning control of his gang, the Gophers. Madden seemed to take a particular pleasure in delivering a savage beating, often using a lead pipe as his weapon of choice. But he wasn't shy with

the gun either. In 1910 Owney shot a man to death on a crowded streetcar. The dead man's offense was apparently trying to date one of Madden's girls. Owney was cleared of the charges when, despite a streetcar full of witnesses, no one was willing to testify against the young thug.

The crimes of the Gophers during that time were generally of the brutal variety—muggings, labor intimidation, and armed robbery. In all, Madden was arrested over forty times before he was twenty-one years old. A shootout with a rival gang in 1912 left Madden with five new holes in his body. Owney survived. Rather than tell the police who had shot him, however, he took matters into

Opposite: Owney Madden in a 1931 New York police mug shot.

Left: The exterior of Harlem's Cotton Club. Madden owned the famous speakeasy, which featured some of the best black entertainers in the country.

Above: 1932: A stylish Owney Madden (left) is escorted by police detective Thomas Horan shortly after the mobster was ordered to return to Sing Sing prison for parole violations.

his own hands and had six members of the rival gang killed. During his absence while Owney recovered, another member of the Gophers, Little Patty Doyle, tried to move into the leadership role. Owney personally took care of the mutiny and shot Doyle to death. Madden was pinched for the murder and sent up the river to Sing Sing, eventually serving eight years on a ten to twenty-year sentence.

Madden emerged from the walls of Sing Sing a more mature, more educated, calmer man. No longer living up to the nickname "the Killer," Owney set about using his wits to get rich, tapping into the huge sums of money to be made in bootlegging illegal alcohol during Prohibition. His rumrunning activities brought him into the major leagues of the mob, wheeling, dealing and sometimes feuding with the likes of Dutch Schultz, Lucky Luciano, and all the usual suspects of the New York underworld.

Madden was also looking for a Harlem venue to sell his beer, *Madden's #1*. He found a speakeasy on Lenox Avenue and 142nd Street called the Club De Luxe, owned by heavyweight boxer Jack Johnson. Madden bought the club from the fighter in 1923 and renamed it the Cotton Club.

The club was a huge hit among its white clientele. Featuring Duke Ellington and his Orchestra as the house band, and the best black entertainers in show business, the Cotton Club was *the* place to rub elbows with the rich and famous and to hear the greatest jazz musicians of the era. The club was very much a product of the times, with light-skinned black entertainers playing to a white-only audience. The décor was a mixture of southern plantation and tropical themes to match the "jungle" music of Ellington and his band. With his income from the club and bootlegging, Owney became very wealthy and influential. Enough so that during a later stint at Sing Sing, he often had Cotton Club entertainers travel up to the prison to perform for him and his fellow inmates.

But all was not roses for Madden. An irritant in the form of Vincent "Mad Dog" Coll was an annoyance to most of

New York's mobsters, Owney in particular. Coll's signature racket was to kidnap mobsters and hold them for ransom. Coll pulled the stunt several times on some of Madden's men, and Owney ponied up the ransom each time. When Coll finally met his end in a bullet-riddled phone booth, he was reportedly talking to Madden, who kept the Mad Dog on the line until mob gunsels ended the conversation.

In 1932 Madden was returned to prison on a parole violation. Upon his release, with Prohibition repealed and the mob looking for new streams of revenue, Owney liquidated all his assets, pulled up roots and moved to Hot Springs, Arkansas, to begin a new life running illegal casinos. Hot Springs, over the years, had been a place for mobsters to go to let legal heat cool down. Owney would play host to many of them. It truly was a new life for Madden, far from the hustle of the Big Apple, the sights and sounds of the Cotton Club, and the bars of Sing Sing. Hot Springs agreed with Owney. The cops and city officials were easily bought and no further legal

Left: Madden (left) leaves Sing Sing with an unidentified man on July 7, 1933 after having served one year for violation of parole on a manslaughter sentence.

troubles befell him. He married the daughter of the local postmaster in 1943 and lived with a certain air of legitimacy and a level of respectability until his death of natural causes in 1965. Owney "the Killer" Madden was one mobster who managed to beat the odds, having lived by the sword and died of old age.

Left: New Year's revelers ring in 1937 at the Cotton Club as Cab Calloway conducts the band. By this time, Owney Madden had already sold the club and moved on to a new life in Hot Springs, Arkansas.

Abner Zwillman

"Zwillman's friends quote him as saying shortly before his death that for years the politicians took his money and said everything would be all right but, 'when I need them not one bastard is around.'"
—From Longie Zwillman's FBI file

A bner "Longie" Zwillman may or may not have committed suicide. At the height of his power he was called the "Al Capone of New Jersey." With a seat on the national Syndicate's governing board, a hand in rackets across the country, the respect of fellow mobsters, millions in annual income, and a reported strong Jewish faith, why would Zwillman kill himself? It's true that he was under indictment for tax evasion, but was that enough to make him hang himself in the basement of his mansion?

Abner Zwillman was born in Newark, New Jersey, in 1904 (although this date is often put earlier). There's no mystery as to the origin of his nickname, "Longie." He stood at 6'2" (nearly a foot taller than his friend Meyer Lansky). There is a story in the Jewish community of New Jersey that whenever there was trouble with Irish gangs, the call in Yiddish would go out for "the tall one." After his father's death, Zwillman had to drop out of high school to get a job to support his large family. He began selling produce from a rented horse and cart in the neighborhoods of Newark. He soon learned that he could supplement his income by offering lottery tickets for numbers rackets to his produce buyers.

Zwillman began to see where the real money was to be made, and it wasn't long before he was controlling the numbers rackets throughout Newark.

The Volstead Act for Longie, as for other mobsters, was a goldmine. Under Prohibition, Zwillman set up an impressive network for importing huge amounts of illicit alcohol from Canada via trucks and boats. He expanded his rackets to include prostitution and gambling as well as nightclubs and restaurants. In the waning days of Prohibition, the national crime Syndicate was formed and Longie was one of the founding members of the Commission.

Zwillman's partner throughout his career in organized crime was Willie Moretti, an interesting character in his own right. Moretti is supposed to be the mobster who gave Frank Sinatra his break by getting the crooner out of his contract with bandleader Tommy Dorsey. Moretti reportedly made Dorsey an offer he couldn't refuse, somehow convincing the bandleader to sell Sinatra's contract for the bargain price of one dollar. Zwillman, too, had connections to show business. Longie is said to have been instrumental in helping Jean Harlow's career by convincing Colombia Pictures head Harry Cohn to give Harlow a two-picture deal.

Opposite: Abner Zwillman at the Federal Courthouse in New York 1939 where he was brought before a grand jury to answer questions regarding fugitive mobster Louis "Lepke" Buchalter. Zwillman refused to answer the questions put to him.

Cohn was apparently returning a favor for Zwillman, who had lent the movie mogul some $500,000. The exact nature of the relationship between Zwillman and Harlow is unclear, but some stories tell of Longie carrying a special lock of Harlow's hair which he would brandish on occasion. He is also reported to have bought the starlet expensive jewelry and a red Cadillac.

In another more infamous brush with fame, Zwillman's name is one of several that are curious footnotes in the tragic and controversial case of the kidnapping of Charles Lindbergh, Jr. After the famous flier's infant son was abducted from the family home in Hopewell, New Jersey, in 1932, police went on a massive manhunt throughout the state, setting up roadblocks which put a significant crimp into the business of local bootleggers. Zwillman offered a substantial reward for the capture of the kidnapper,

perhaps out of genuine concern, or perhaps in order to hasten the end of the crippling roadblocks.

Abner Zwillman is also reported to have organized the hit on Dutch Schultz in 1935. While Schultz was in upstate New York fighting the government on charges of tax evasion, his lieutenant, Bo Weinberg, was busy selling him out to the Syndicate. Assuming that the Dutchman was going to be sent to prison for the long haul, Weinberg decided to give over Schultz's empire to the national criminal coalition, which quickly divided up the territory among various gangs, with Longie picking up much of the Dutchman's operations in New Jersey. But Schultz beat the tax rap and was soon looking for payback, most notably by asking the Commission if he could whack the crusading prosecutor, Thomas E. Dewey. The idea was vetoed, but the Dutchman vowed to carry out the high profile hit anyway. Before he could carry out his plan, however, he was shot to death in a restaurant in Newark, Zwillman's home territory.

Zwillman's political connections were formidable. Through bribes and political contributions, Longie was able to practically pick and choose governors, and by extension, all gubernatorial appointees,

---

VITAL SIGNS

Born: July 27, 1904
Died: February 27, 1959
Cause of Death: Suicide
Buried: Temple B'nai Abraham Memorial Park; Union, New Jersey

including state attorney generals. But despite all his political clout in New Jersey, Zwillman was not able to remain immune from federal criminal scrutiny. Zwillman had always tried to keep a low profile as a mobster, while publicly posing as a legitimate businessman. But in the late 1950s, the McClellan Committee, a Senate subcommittee investigating organized crime, subpoenaed Zwillman to appear, shattering Longie's façade of legitimacy. At the same time there was an investigation into his finances by the Internal Revenue Service. Zwillman was facing the fate that had befallen many mobsters before him, that of a long prison sentence for tax evasion.

One of two things happened next. The generally accepted scenario is that a distraught Zwillman, unable to bear the prospect of years spent behind bars in federal prison, killed himself. The other theory is that a distraught Zwillman, unable to bear the prospect of years spent behind bars in federal prison, decided to cut a deal with prosecutors. The Commission, not wanting to hear what Longie had to say, had Zwillman exe-

Left: James Cagney and Jean Harlow in the classic 1931 gangster film The Public Enemy. *Zwillman is said to have aided Harlow's early career.*

cuted, making it look like a suicide. It has been reported that there were signs of struggle that were conveniently overlooked by homicide investigators, but much can be made out of little when a good conspiracy theory is in the balance. Either way, Abner Zwillman was found dead, hanging by the neck in the basement of his West Orange mansion, on February 27, 1959.

Left: Zwillman (left) in 1951 conferring with attorney Arthur G. Hayes.

Albert Anastasia

"I ate from the same table as Albert and came from the same womb, but I know he killed many men and deserved to die."
—ANTHONY "TOUGH TONY" ANASTASIO, BROTHER OF ALBERT

lbert Anastasia's story can be summed up in one of his nicknames, "The Lord High Executioner." From his early days as a Brooklyn longshoreman, through his ascent to the top of one of New York's five crime families, Anastasia cleaved a path of death and terror that finally ended with bullets in a barber's chair. A fitting end for the mob's "Mad Hatter."

Umberto Anastasio was born in Calabria, Italy, on February 26, 1902. One of five children, he emigrated at a young age to the United States, along with other family members, including older brother Anthony. Arriving in the ports of New York City around 1917, Anastasio soon became known as Albert Anastasia, although his brother and family would keep their original surname. Albert and his brother began working as longshoremen where toughness was a prerequisite. It wasn't long before Albert began his career as a killer as well. In 1920, a rabblerouser who had been stirring up labor unrest at the docks showed up a murder victim. Anastasia was arrested in connection, convicted and sentenced to death. That may have been the end of Albert Anastasia, barely a footnote in history, but an appeal by his lawyers was granted on a technicality. Curiously, the four witnesses who had testified against Anastasia in the first trial were all not-so-coincidentally murdered. With no witnesses against him, in April of 1922, Anastasia was

released from death row and back onto the streets of New York, a free man.

It was a New York City crime reporter who coined the name "Murder, Inc." for the enforcement arm of the national crime Syndicate. There is some question as to the makeup and organization of Murder, Inc., but most sources hold that Albert Anastasia was one of its leaders, along with Louis Lepke (aka Louis Buchalter). Among the Murder, Inc., ranks were Abe "Kid Twist" Reles, Happy Maione, "Pittsburgh Phil" Strauss, as well as a host of other professional and part-time killers alike. Murder, Inc., was credited with many hundreds of mob hits over the years, with many ascribed either directly or indirectly to Anastasia. A King's County District Attorney put Albert's personal death toll at seventeen between 1930 and 1939, alone. Techniques of the professional killers ranged from ice picks in the ear to bullets in the brain, from strangling to stabbing, even burying victims alive.

One member of Murder, Inc., would be the undoing of the organization itself, landing several fellow members in the electric chair. After a few of the organization's killers were picked up by the cops for murder and started singing, Abe "Kid Twist" Reles saw the handwriting on the wall and decided to flip on his old pals, either to save himself from the electric chair, or to soothe a murder-filled conscience. He turned himself in and his tes-

Opposite: Albert Anastasia, seen here in 1954, was known alternately as the "Mad Hatter" and the "Lord High Executioner." Anastasia's nicknames were derived from his violent and unpredictable nature.

Right: Anastasia's description and personal information from the back of his 1936 police mug shot. It is uncertain what type of oil Anastasia claimed to be selling.

Opposite, bottom: Anastasia's body on the floor of Grasso's Barber Shop inside the Park Sheraton Hotel on Seventh Avenue and 56th Street in Manhattan. The hotel had also been the site of Arnold Rothstein's shooting in 1928 when the hotel was called the Park Central Hotel.

Opposite, top: Albert Anastasia's 1936 New York Police Department mug shot.

```
POLICE DEPARTMENT
CITY OF NEW YORK          No.

Name    Albert Amastasio
Alias
Residence  387 Clinton St Bkly
Crime   Vagrancy
Age     34--1936    Height  5D9
Weight  202         Build
Hair    Brown       Eyes    Brown
Color   White       Comp.   Dark
Born    Italy
Occupation  Oil Salesman
Date of Arrest
Officer
Remarks

        27      11
        28      01      19
F. P. CLASS
```

timony gave Louis Lepke the dubious honor of being the only mob boss ever to die in the electric chair. In the process, Kid Twist signed his own death warrant. With Anastasia next in line on Reles's song list, a curious thing happened. While in police protective custody, Abe Reles was found dead one morning in 1941 after having taken a one-way trip out of a sixth-floor hotel window. How he got there, either by himself or with help (and in the midst of six cops who were sworn to protect him), remains a mystery. Either way, Albert Anastasia managed, once again, to escape the chair.

─── **SCREEN TIME** ───

Lansky (1999). Played by Nick Corello
Lepke (1975). Played by Gianni Russo
The Valachi Papers (1972). Played by Fausto Tozzi
Murder, Inc. (1960). Played by Howard I. Smith

Throughout much of his career in the mob, Anastasia served as underboss to Vincent Mangano in what would later become the Gambino crime family. Anastasia was also close with Mangano rivals Lucky Luciano and Frank Costello, two of the most powerful men in the Syndicate. Tensions began to arise between Mangano and Anastasia in the early 1950s. Perhaps Anastasia's relationship with Costello made Mangano suspicious. As it turned out, he probably had good reason to be suspicious. In April of 1951, both Vincent Mangano and his brother Philip went missing. Philip's body was eventually discovered in a marsh near Coney Island with gunshots to the head. Vincent's body was never found, though his grieving family didn't have him declared officially dead until ten years later. One story has it that he's part of a building foundation somewhere in Brooklyn. Regardless of his final resting place, Vincent Mangano was succeeded by his probable killer, the Lord High Executioner himself.

If Albert Anastasia had been murderous and brutal before, his reign as head of one of New York's crime families was a continuation, if not an escalation, of his violent ways. Take for example the case of Arnold Schuster. A Brooklyn men's wear salesman with no connection to organized crime, Schuster's brush with the Mad Hatter came in 1952, when Schuster recognized the infamous bank robber, Willie Sutton, walking down the street and turned him in to the police. Schuster's deed brought him some notoriety, including a fateful television interview that was seen by Anastasia. "I hate squealers. Hit that guy," Albert A. was remembered as

─── **VITAL SIGNS** ───

Born: February 26, 1902
Died: October 25, 1957
Cause of Death: Murdered (shot)
Buried: Green-Wood Cemetery; Brooklyn, New York

saying. The hit, carried out in March of 1952, crossed a line that was part of the code of mobsters: "We only kill each other," as Bugsy Siegel had put it. Unless the well being of the family was in jeopardy, those outside the mob were off limits. Anastasia, however, may have felt that such rules did not apply to him.

In 1954, Anastasia was indicted for tax evasion by the Feds. The first trial ended in a hung jury after one witness was found dead in the trunk of his car, and another was never found at all. The second trial went much the same way with yet another witness and his wife discovered missing from their blood-spattered home. However, perhaps seeing an opportunity to deflect further legal troubles, Anastasia pled guilty to tax evasion. The Mad Hatter was given a virtual slap on the wrist with a year in federal prison in Michigan. It was only the second time that Anastasia served any time in jail since his days on death row over twenty years before.

In 1957, Anastasia reached his term limit as head of his crime family. Perhaps it was because he had broken another rule of mob code by selling memberships into the crime family for $50,000 each. Or perhaps it was that he was so unpredictable and dangerous as to be a liability to the other families. Or perhaps it was one element of a power play by the ambitious Vito Genovese. Whatever the reason, on the morning of October 25, 1957, Albert Anastasia would finally meet his Maker in the chair, although not the chair he might have expected.

His usual bodyguard conspicuously absent, Anastasia sat relaxing under hot towels in a barber chair in the Park Sheraton Hotel in Manhattan. Two men walked in and opened fire with .38 pistols. When they walked out, Albert Anastasia was dead, shot several times in the body and hands, once through the head. Although many names and theories were floated, the hitmen were never definitively identified, nor were those who contracted the hit. It is generally believed that it was done by order of Anastasia's own underboss, Carlo Gambino (who, many believe, was acting at the behest of Vito Genovese). Gambino would inherit the family that would infamously bear his name. But whoever was responsible for the hit had a flair for the dramatic and ensured that the Lord High Executioner died as he had lived.

Mobsters in the Military

Many mobsters served their country, with varying degrees of willingness and success. In 1942, Albert Anastasia was drafted into the army and rose to the rank of technical sergeant, although he served domestically, seeing no combat. Jack "Legs" Diamond was drafted into the army in 1918 and immediately went AWOL, and instead served two years at Leavenworth. Moe Dalitz served in the army in the 1940s, rising to the rank of second lieutenant. Al Capone never served in the military, although he often claimed that he received his famous facial scars serving in the "Lost Battalion" during World War I. Lucky Luciano never served in the military either, but was granted parole from prison for his role in helping to thwart German saboteurs and for providing intelligence for the Allied invasion of Italy during World War II. Vito Genovese also helped the Allies in Italy, acting as a translator for the U.S. Army, all the while stealing army goods and selling them on the black market. Joe Colombo served in the Coast Guard, but was reportedly given a medical discharge for "psychoneurosis."

Mickey Cohen

"I have killed no man that in the first place didn't deserve killing by the standards of our way of life."

—Mickey Cohen in an interview with reporter Mike Wallace

There were mobsters who preferred to be in the shadows, keeping their faces off of television and out of newspapers, realizing that publicity was bad for business. Then there were the mobsters who enjoyed the limelight. They lived large, actively seeking the limelight and flaunting their lawlessness before all. Such a mobster was Mickey Cohen.

Meyer Harris Cohen was born in Brownsville, Brooklyn, in 1913. The Cohen family moved to Los Angeles when little Mickey was six years old, where they owned and operated a drug store. The Volstead Act called for the prohibition of the manufacture and sale of alcohol, but made limited exception for the distilling of alcohol for medicinal purposes. The Cohen's drug store, therefore, was an ideal cover for their small gin mill, which they used to make and distribute alcohol, medicinal and otherwise. Little Mickey learned at an early age how to work around the law in order to make a buck.

Cohen never did grow to be very big—he was 5'5" in wingtips. But what he lacked in size, he made up for in toughness. Mickey got into boxing at an early age. He did well in the ring, winning local matches and earning some prize money. Bolstered by his success, Mickey decided to go east to try his hands at becoming a pro. A decisive loss in New York, to featherweight world

champion Tommy Paul, changed Mickey's mind. He decided to put his fists to work in something more familiar. Mickey began robbing nightclubs and illegal gambling casinos, apparently unaware that the joints he was sticking up were owned by mobsters. The mob was always looking for new talent, though, so instead of taking Mickey out, they took him in.

Cohen, in his early mob career, met and worked for many of the big names of the Syndicate, moving around to different outfits in New York, Chicago and Cleveland, eventually landing back in Los Angeles working under Benjamin "Bugsy" Siegel. The Syndicate had moved Siegel out to the West Coast in the late 1930s to both diffuse tensions (as well as legal trouble) brought about by Siegel's violent personality, and to set up

Opposite: Mickey Cohen in Chicago waves to the camera as he heads out of town in 1950. Police arrested Cohen because they didn't "want to find his body on a Chicago street." Cohen survived several attempts on his life by rival Los Angeles mobster Jack Dragna.

Below: Cohen in an L.A. police station in 1959 was brought in for questioning regarding a murder in a local restaurant. He listed his occupation as "associate author" without further explanation.

Right: Mickey Cohen (right) being interviewed by journalist Mike Wallace in 1957. Cohen claimed that he had reformed and purported to be a school teacher and florist.

Opposite, bottom: *Mickey Cohen (right) with Johnny Stompanato in 1950. Stompanato was stabbed to death in the home of his girlfriend Lana Turner in 1958.*

a base of operations in California. The boss in L.A. at the time was Jack Dragna, who was unaffiliated with the eastern Syndicate. He reluctantly decided that it would be better to allow the easterners into the state than to try to fight them. But his resentment simmered.

Bugsy Siegel had the lifestyle of a celebrity, hobnobbing with the Hollywood set, and maintaining a high profile in the press. Mickey Cohen enjoyed the limelight generated by his boss. When Bugsy moved to Las Vegas in the early 1940s to build the Flamingo Hotel and Casino, Cohen took over much of the operation of the Syndicate's business in his stead. Upon Siegel's mob-ordered murder in 1947, Cohen was offi-

cially put in charge of all operations, and Dragna's resentment boiled over. Cohen would become the target of no fewer than five assassination attempts over the following years. He survived all of them through a combination of luck and incompetence on the part of his would-be assassins. This incompetence led in part to the West Coast mob's nickname, the "Mickey Mouse Mafia."

Assassination tries on Cohen's life included shooting attempts as well as a couple of bombing attempts. One bomb was placed in the basement of Cohen's home. However, it had been placed beneath a re-enforced concrete safe and the resulting explosion did more damage to a neighbor's home than to Cohen's. Another attempt, seemingly out of a bad Hollywood comedy, had bullets whizzing past Cohen's head as he bent down to check a ding in his Cadillac. In each attempt, Cohen was left unhurt and very much alive.

Mickey Cohen had extensive contacts within Hollywood and the press. He was reportedly acquainted with newspaper mogul William Randolph Hearst and did television interviews with the likes of Mike Wallace. He was friends with studio heads as well as celebrities, like Rat Packers Frank Sinatra and Sammy Davis, Jr. Cohen reportedly prevented a hit (requested by Columbia Pictures head Harry Cohn) on Davis for his dating

--- VITAL SIGNS ---

Born: 1913
Died: 1976
Cause of Death: Natural causes
Buried: Hillside Memorial Park; Culver City, California

--- SCREEN TIME ---

The Rat Pack (1998) (TV). Played by Alan Woolf
Bugsy (1991). Played by Harvey Keitel

white actress Kim Novak. But Mickey's brush with actress Lana Turner was particularly infamous. Johnny Stompanato, a long-time friend of Cohen's (some say his bodyguard), had a stormy relationship with the actress that eventually led to the stabbing death of Stompanato by Turner's fourteen-year-old daughter, Cheryl Crane. However, Crane was eventually acquitted of the crime, and the relationship between Turner and Cohen grew publicly rancorous. Cohen even gave the press love letters written by Turner to Stompanato. It was said that Turner would go out of her way to avoid Cohen because she feared for her life.

Cohen went to prison twice, both times on tax evasion charges. The second time, in 1962, was particularly difficult for Mickey, when he served ten years of a fifteen-year sentence. Part of that time was spent in Alcatraz, which Cohen referred to as a "crumbling dungeon." He emerged from prison in 1972 a changed man, both physically and mentally. Partially paralyzed from an attack by a fellow inmate, Cohen got around with the help of a walker and declared himself retired. Yet despite his retirement from crime, he would have two more forays into the public eye before his death.

The kidnapping of newspaper heiress Patricia Hearst would lead the Hearst family to seek help from Mickey Cohen. In 1974, the Symbionese Liberation Army, a group of American terrorists who sought to wage war on capitalism, abducted Patty Hearst, heiress to the Hearst publishing empire. Cohen, through old mob and prison contacts, claimed to have tracked Hearst down in Cleveland, but dropped out of the search when he realized that Hearst might face prosecution for her involvement with the SLA. Cohen, now old and in ill health, did not want to be involved with anything that might jeopardize his parole and send him back to prison.

In 1975, Cohen published his memoirs, *Mickey Cohen: In My Own Words*. The book gave great insight into the life of a Hollywood mobster. The following year the man who had survived so many attempts on his life died of natural causes in his home in Los Angeles. He was sixty-three years old.

Owning Hollywood

Similar to labor rackets in other industries, the mob managed to command significant power in Hollywood by controlling its unions. Mobsters like Bugsy Siegel and Mickey Cohen extorted money from movie moguls by either threatening strikes that would keep movie extras off sets, or collecting cash from those same moguls to intimidate the unions into averting strikes. It was a classic racket that played both sides against the middle. It worked for Louis "Lepke" Buchalter in the garment and baking industries in New York. And it worked just as well in the studios of Hollywood. Only in Hollywood, the mobsters were controlling the stars.

Above: Hollywood, California, 1958. The famous sign was erected in 1923.

Moe Dalitz

"Dixie Davis stated Moe Davis (aka Moe Dalitz) was a 'power' in Cleveland between 1931 and 1936. Dixie Davis wrote, 'Moey Davis became the power in Cleveland and anyone who questioned it would have to deal with Lucky, Meyer and Bug.'"
—FBI REPORT QUOTING AUGUST 14, 1939, *Collier's* MAGAZINE ARTICLE

If Moe Dalitz was unknown in the Pantheon of mobster names, he probably would have preferred it that way. But his success as a businessman, both legitimate and otherwise, was equal to any mobster around. By the time of Dalitz's death in 1989 at the ripe old age of eighty-nine, he was widely regarded by many in the Las Vegas area as a gentleman and a great philanthropist, as well as one of the founding fathers of Sin City. His long life in and around the mob was not forgotten but mostly forgiven. Moe Dalitz's story is not only a mob success story, but also the story of a man who transcended the mob.

Born in Boston on December 24, 1899, Morris Barney Dalitz was the son of a laundry operator. After his family moved to Michigan, Moe, as he was called, joined up with a group of Jewish mobsters known as the Purple Gang. During Prohibition, Moe did what most mobsters did: smuggled booze. After a move to Cleveland, Moe joined the Mayfield Road Gang. There he teamed up with some of the up-and-coming young Italian mobsters, and helped them to move in on the old-time Mustache Petes who had been running the show, much the way Meyer Lansky and Lucky Luciano were doing in New York. The new way of doing business overlooked old ethnic divides for the benefits that could be gained by working together.

After Prohibition was repealed, Dalitz moved into the gambling business, operating illegal gambling houses in Ohio, Kentucky, Florida, and other surrounding states. But running illegal businesses was not without its risks—they were *illegal,* after all. After learning how much money there was to be made in the casino business, Moe began looking into places where gambling was legal. Meyer Lansky was making a big bet on Cuba to be America's foremost gambling destination. Dalitz covered his bets by investing in both Cuba and Nevada casinos, but when the Nevada gambling commission decided to deny operating licenses to anyone involved in Cuban casinos, Dalitz opted to lay his money on Las Vegas. As it turned out, Dalitz made the right bet. When Fidel Castro overthrew the regime of Fulgencio Batista in Cuba in 1959, he confiscated American-owned businesses in

Opposite: Las Vegas casino mogul and former bootlegger Moe Dalitz in 1963.

Above: The Vegas Strip in 1970. In the foreground is the Flamingo Hotel and Casino. In the background can be seen the Sands, Frontier and Stardust Casinos.

Opposite, bottom: Tale of Two Sin Cities: the Stardust Casino in 1970 (top) and the Vegas Strip on January 1, 2003.

Opposite, top: Eccentric billionaire Howard Hughes in 1947.

the name of the people's revolution, and fortunes invested in the Havana casinos were lost.

In 1950 Dalitz bought the Desert Inn Casino in Las Vegas. It was also at this time that Estes Kefauver came to town with his committee investigating organized crime in America. Dalitz was compelled to testify before the committee, and held his own against questioning, replying to a Kefauver query about how he made his money in his early years, "Well, I didn't inherit any money, Senator. If

---

VITAL SIGNS

Born: December 24, 1899
Died: 1989
Cause of Death: Natural causes

SCREEN TIME

Lansky (1999) (TV). Played by Peter Siragusa

---

you people wouldn't have drunk it, I wouldn't have bootlegged it." In all, Dalitz was indicted only twice in his life, once for bootlegging in 1930, and another time for tax evasion in 1965. Both indictments were dismissed.

In 1958, Moe Dalitz bought the Stardust Casino. It was being built with mob money by gambler Tony Cornero. Cornero was in debt to the mob to the tune of $6 million dollars, and was in negotiations with Dalitz to have the Stardust brought into his organization, when Cornero dropped dead on the gambling floor of the Desert Inn. An autopsy was never performed. Cornero's death was convenient for Dalitz, who promptly arranged to buy the Stardust at a much more reasonable rate than what Cornero was asking.

Moe was more than just a tough businessman. He was just plain tough. One story tells of the heavyweight boxer, Sonny Liston, drunkenly threatening to punch the mobster after an altercation in a Hollywood restaurant.

Dalitz calmly and quietly warned the fighter, "If you hit me, you'd better kill me, because if you don't, I'll make one telephone call and you'll be dead in twenty-four hours." Dalitz also threw in a racial epithet that could have easily incited the boxer to violence. But Liston apparently thought better of it and walked away without further incident. Moe Dalitz had stared down the heavyweight champion of the world.

After a tax evasion indictment was dismissed in 1965, Dalitz, perhaps looking to avoid further legal problems, sold the Desert Inn to eccentric billionaire Howard Hughes, who offered to settle his gambling debts by buying the casino. Throughout his long career, however, Dalitz kept his hand in a great many legitimate businesses as well as his illegal activities, and in the process had accrued a great deal of cash and clout. He had influence with Nevada politicians as well as with Jimmy Hoffa and the Teamsters Union. In his later years, Dalitz also gave much back to the community, building hospitals and donating to the University of Nevada, Las Vegas, and numerous charities and non-profit organizations. He was even named Humanitarian of the Year by the American Cancer Research Center and Hospital in 1976.

Moe Dalitz died in 1989. He lived a long and varied life. In his eighty-nine years, he traveled from bootlegger to mobster to casino mogul to respectable businessman. He is still respected and honored today as a philanthropist and as a founding father of the Vegas Strip.

Howard Hughes

After buying the Desert Inn, Howard Hughes went on a shopping spree, purchasing the Sands, Frontier, Silver Slipper, and Landmark Casinos, and was prevented by the SEC from buying the Stardust, for fear that Hughes was trying to set up a monopoly on gambling in Nevada. (He'd also bought a casino in Reno.) Hughes bought the CBS television affiliate in Las Vegas in order to control the late night movie programming that he loved to watch, and he purchased the North Las Vegas Airport with plans to build a new, bigger airport. This spend-fest is often portrayed as a noble attempt to "de-mob" Las Vegas. If that's the case, the attempt was indeed ambitious. All told, Hughes is thought to have spent over $300 million in Las Vegas, with his casinos accounting for seventeen percent of Nevada's gambling revenue. He also gave generously to politicians. Among the requests in return for political contributions was a law which exempted Howard Hughes from being forced to appear in any court, and a law prohibiting the realignment of Vegas streets without Hughes' approval. People joked that they were changing the name of Las Vegas to Hugheston.

Meyer Lansky

"Meyer Lansky and his group skimmed more money than anybody in the world. From Las Vegas alone, they got 300 million easy."
—JIMMY "THE WEASEL" FRATIANNO

There is a well-known maxim in gambling that says, "The house always wins." It was a simple truth that Meyer Lansky knew well. From his early days of nickel bets on sidewalk crap games on the Lower East Side of New York, to illegal carpet joints across the United States in later years, the rule always proved true. So in 1957 it was natural for Lansky to assume that it was a safe bet to open a multi-million dollar hotel-casino in Cuba. Meyer placed his wager and invested blood, sweat and tears, not to mention significant capital in gambling in the Caribbean country. But this time the house lost.

On August 28, 1900, Meyer Suchowljansky was born in Grodno, Poland, into a Jewish family. But as anti-semitic oppression intensified at the start of the century, many Jews left in search of a better life, among them the Suchowljansky family. They arrived in New York in 1911 at Ellis Island, where Meyer's year of birth was mistakenly recorded as 1902. The family settled first in Brooklyn, then later on Manhattan's Lower East Side. By the time Meyer and his younger brother Jake began attending school in their newly adopted homeland, their Polish surnames were shortened to a more manageable Lansky.

Young Meyer excelled in school, quickly learning English, and skipping through grades, while showing a particular talent for mathematics. Life on Manhattan's Lower East Side in the early part of the 20th century was a study in vice. Prostitution, muggings and gambling were in full view for the young Meyer, who was captivated by the sidewalk crap games. His gift for numbers led Lansky to believe that he could beat the odds, and one day he bet the nickel given to him by his mother for the Sabbath dinner on a roll of the dice. He promptly lost that nickel, but sensing that there was

Opposite: 1928 New York Police Department mug shot of Meyer Lansky. He listed his profession as "auto mechanic."

Left: Godfather knows best: Lansky waits to testify in 1975 before a Fort Lauderdale, Florida, grand jury investigating illegal gambling in the state.

something he had missed in his calculations, vowed to win it back. Further study of the crap games showed Meyer that there was more at work than just odds. There was also a scam. Shills working in concert with the house would win enough to entice easy marks into the game, thus suckering them into rolling the loaded dice, and out of the money in their pockets. It was clear to Meyer that the only winners in these games were those who controlled them. Lansky decided that he wanted to be in control.

Meyer left school at the age of fifteen and began working in a machine shop, but spent his spare time learning a different trade, that of an aspiring mobster. He amassed a big bankroll hosting crap games and serving as muscle in labor disputes. Along the way he met young toughs who would become friends and partners, like Charlie "Lucky" Luciano and Benjamin "Bugsy" Siegel. He also met Arnold Rothstein, the legendary gambler and underworld financier who reportedly took the young Lansky under his wing, and helped to finance the early bootlegging operations of the Bug and Meyer Mob. Named for Lansky and his partner Bugsy Siegel, the gang headquartered out of a Brooklyn car and truck rental business that handily fronted their rumrunning activities. The Bug and Meyer Mob thrived during Prohibition, importing illegal alcohol and purportedly offering an enforcement service to other gangs that would later serve as the model for the infamous Murder, Inc.

For Meyer Lansky and Lucky Luciano, as with many mobsters, the Castellammarese War and the specter of Repeal presented a crossroads. As the Roaring '20s drew to a close, it was clear to many that the Prohibition gravy train would soon end, and that territorial gang wars, like those in Chicago, would only serve to endanger the lavish lifestyles to which the mobsters had become accustomed. Crime needed to both organize and diversify. It was Luciano and Lansky who led the way, first eliminating those who stood in the way of organization, then putting in place the structure and ground rules for the new nationally organized crime coalition known as the Syndicate. Luciano and Lansky were members of the Commission, the ruling body of the Syndicate, along with various heads of gangs across the

country. The Commission made decisions concerning the various members of the Syndicate, but mostly stood to ensure peace and prosperity in the underworld.

By the time Repeal came in 1933, Meyer Lansky was already heavily invested in the racket that had given him his start, gambling. There were few other rackets that offered the same profit margin, and also the level of respectability. Lansky gradually acquired interests in illegal casinos in New York, Arkansas, Kentucky, Louisiana, and Florida, and in legal casinos in Nevada, most notably Bugsy Siegel's pet project, the Flamingo, in Las Vegas. The lavish hotel-casino opened in 1946, but with such significant cost overruns that Siegel was suspected of skimming construction costs. Bugsy Siegel was executed in a mob hit in 1947, some say ordered by Lansky himself.

But for all of his involvement in legal and illegal gambling, Meyer Lansky somehow managed for many years to mostly fly under the radar of law enforcement. He was often misidentified in investigations or overlooked altogether. The Kefauver Committee, investigating illegal gambling in the United States in the early 1950s, called Lansky to testify three times, but never before cameras and in the end, didn't get much information beyond his recitation of the Fifth Amendment. However, one of Meyer's secrets to success was his ability to remain in shadow, and the Kefauver hearings brought Lansky a level of public exposure that he had always sought to avoid. Following the hearings, he was convicted of a gambling charge related to his interests in casinos in Saratoga Springs, New York, and ended up serving three months in jail. Once he was identified as one of the top crime bosses of the Syndicate, there was no place to hide—except maybe ninety miles off of Florida's southern coast.

In 1952, Fulgencio Batista reclaimed the Cuban presidency and set out on a campaign to increase tourism to his country. Ironically, one of the first steps by the corrupt Batista was to clean up rampant cor-

ruption in the casinos. Batista turned to a man who had a reputation for running straight high-stakes operations, Meyer Lansky. Batista employed Lansky as a paid government advisor, and together the men began to transform Cuba into a respectable and desirable destination for gamblers and tourists. Lansky had secret investments in Las Vegas casinos, but he saw in Cuba the opportunity to create a Caribbean gambling oasis that he could essentially monopolize. He opened a casino in the historic Hotel Nacional in 1955, before beginning construction on his own hotel-casino.

The Riviera opened in Havana in late 1957. It was an immediate success, offering honest gambling and opulent surroundings with Meyer reportedly taking a personal interest in the kitchens to ensure that the cuisine was the best on the island. Hotel-casinos began sprouting up, with many more in the works, but all had to go through Meyer Lansky first. Where Las Vegas casinos were open to anyone with the capital, Lansky virtually owned gambling in Cuba.

All bets were off when a new political era dawned in Cuba in the wee hours of New Year's Day, 1959. Fearful of popular rebellion and under pressure to step down as president of Cuba, Batista fled his country at midnight on December 31, 1958. Meyer Lansky was apparently taken by surprise by the news, and it quickly became apparent that the new leader in Cuba, Fidel Castro, would not allow the casinos to operate. Having not yet recouped his investments on the Riviera and other projects, Meyer Lansky was forced to flee Cuba and swallow his losses. It was the first time in Lansky's experience that the house lost, and lost big.

The fiasco in Cuba by no means ruined Meyer Lansky. He did take a significant hit, however, both financially and emotionally. Having devoted so much of time, money, and energy in Havana, Lansky began showing the strain. He had ulcers and began to develop chest pains, eventually suffering a heart attack some eighteen months after he was kicked out of

---

VITAL SIGNS

Born: August 28, 1900 (often put at 1902)
Died: January 15, 1983
Cause of Death: Natural causes (lung cancer)
Buried: Mt. Nebo Cemetery; Miami, Florida

SCREEN TIME

Lansky (1999) (TV). Played by Richard Dreyfuss
Mobsters, (1991). Played by Patrick Dempsey
Bugsy (1991). Played by Ben Kingsley

Left: Fidel Castro (second left) in 1959. Behind him is a mural depicting ousted Cuban dictator Fulgencio Batista.

Below: Rioters burn roulette tables outside the Plaza Hotel Casino in Havana shortly after Castro's revolutionaries took over power in Cuba. American investors, Lansky included, were forced to leave the country.

Cuba. Following the Kefauver hearings, Lansky was mostly able to avoid the scrutiny of American law enforcement by spending most of his time in Cuba. But now, back in the United States, the FBI was following Meyer's every move, shadowing him everywhere he went and bugging his home. The constant attention of the FBI finally proved too much for the ailing Lansky, and in the 1970s, he decided to leave the United States for what he believed to be the open arms of Israel, which had a right of return law that allowed anyone with a Jewish mother to return to the ancestral homeland.

Following a three-year legal battle which culminated in a decision by the Israeli Supreme Court, Meyer Lansky was ultimately denied permission to live in the country and was ordered to leave. He returned to the United States where the Internal Revenue Service brought tax evasion charges against him. But Meyer had always done well to hide his illegal income, living modestly, leaving no paper trails and keeping business

partnerships silent. The IRS case fell apart, and Meyer was acquitted.

Meyer Lansky died of natural causes on January 15, 1983, in his home in Miami, Florida. At the time of his death he was eighty-three years old, and had served only a grand total of three months in prison, despite a long and prosperous career as a mobster and as one of the masterminds of organized crime in the United States.

Lucky Luciano

"The vice industry, since Luciano took over, is highly organized and operates with businesslike precision."
—PROSECUTOR THOMAS E. DEWEY

One of the most notorious mobsters of all time, Charles "Lucky" Luciano was languishing in a prison in far upstate New York. He had served five years of a thirty to fifty-year sentence, convicted on over sixty counts of compulsory prostitution. He wouldn't even be eligible to face a parole board for another fifteen years. It was possible he might never even live to see the outside world where he had once been so powerful. But all that changed in late 1941, when America was forcibly dragged into World War II. The United States Navy decided that, in order to protect the homeland from German sabotage, it needed the help of Lucky Luciano.

Salvatore Lucania was born in Lercardia Friddi, Sicily, on November 24, 1897. His family sought out a new life in America, settling on Manhattan's Lower East Side in 1906. The young Salvatore was quick to choose his path in life, garnering an arrest for shoplifting in 1907. From there he was soon involved in various rackets from drug dealing to protection, meeting many underworld characters along the way, including Frank Costello, Joe Adonis, Benjamin Siegel, and a smart, young Jewish tough from the neighborhood, Meyer Lansky. One apocryphal story of their first meeting tells of Lucania and a group of his thugs mugging people in the streets of the neighborhood, when one particularly small Jewish boy fought back and told Lucania and his pals what particular act they might perform on themselves. The story describes Lucania being impressed by the youngster's mettle, recognizing a kindred spirit. The two became fast friends, with a life-long, mutual respect.

Before long, Salvatore Lucania was well known in the community, going by the name of Charles Luciano. It is not clear how he arrived at the new name, but he also added his famous nickname somewhere along the way. One mob legend has Charlie Lucky picking up his moniker for being one

Opposite: Former mob kingpin Lucky Luciano smoking in Italy, circa 1950.

Left: Luciano (right) with unidentified man in the back of a police van transporting him from his trial for compulsory prostitution in 1936.

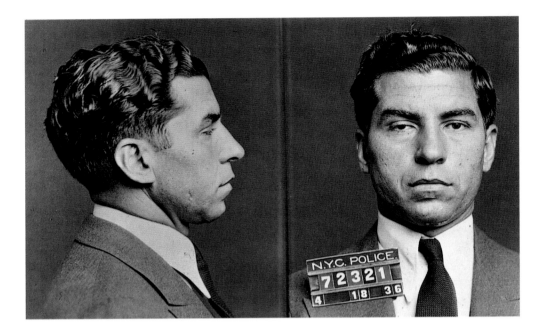

of the few people to survive having been "taken for a ride" by rival mobsters. However, it's more likely that "Lucky" was derived from his original surname that was apparently pronounced with a *k* rather than a *ch* sound. Wherever his new names came from, they would soon be spoken with fear and awe.

By the time Prohibition became law in the United States, Lucky Luciano was working his way up through the ranks of Giuseppe "Joe the Boss" Masseria's organization. He was Masseria's number two in the late 1920s when a tough Mafioso from Italy, Salvatore Maranzano, arrived in New York and immediately set about trying to establish himself as *capo di tutti capi* (boss of bosses) in America. The Mafia in Italy, known as the

---

VITAL SIGNS

Born: November 24, 1897
Died: January 26, 1962
Cause of Death: Natural causes (heart attack)
Buried: St. Johns Cemetery; Queens, New York

Honored Society, was an exclusive organization that shunned doing business with anyone but their own kind. But "their own kind" might exclude anyone who hailed from the next village over, let alone anyone from another country or of a different religion. This sort of jingoism was anathema to the new generation of mobsters like Lucky Luciano and Meyer Lansky, who believed that the principal goal of their endeavors should be to make money. Squabbling over race and religion was simply counterproductive and diminished profits.

While Masseria and Maranzano fought what was later called the Castellammarese War, Luciano, Lansky, and their various like-minded associates made plans of their own. After secretly switching his allegiance to Maranzano in 1931, Luciano had Masseria killed. He arranged a lunch with Masseria and, at the appointed hour, excused himself to go to the bathroom, returning only after the shooting was over and Masseria was dead. Salvatore Maranzano took the opportunity to throw a party at the very same restaurant where Joe the Boss was murdered, the Nuova Villa Tammaro in Coney

Island, and announced that he was now the undisputed *capo di tutti capi* for organized crime in America. However, his self-proclaimed reign didn't last long. Five months after Joe the Boss was killed, Lucky Luciano had Maranzano murdered in his Park Avenue office. The Castellammarese War was officially over.

Charlie Luciano did not invent the national crime Syndicate. The idea and much of the planning for the organization were already in the works when Luciano forcibly took over the heading of its formation in 1931. Salvatore Maranzano had already introduced the idea of crime "families" controlling territories and had assigned or endorsed leadership positions. However, he had also appointed himself as the boss of the whole works. Lucky Luciano knew the resentment that such a position generated and decided to do away with the title altogether. Instead,

---

SCREEN TIME

Hoodlum (1997). Played by Andy Garcia
Mobsters (1991). Played by Christian Slater
Billy Bathgate (1991). Played by Stanley Tucci
Lepke (1975). Played by Vic Tayback

---

each member of the Commission, comprised of heads of the various crime families across the country, voted equally on matters concerning the Syndicate. With the decision-making power spread out, there was no single head of the Syndicate to whom tribute was paid, which meant that there was no one man who might incur the wrath of disgruntled members or be subject to intense legal scrutiny. In short, crime in America became organized.

Left: Luciano (center wearing hat), handcuffed to detectives, is led out of courtroom on June 18, 1936, after receiving a thirty to fifty-year sentence for vice crimes.

Right: Luciano pouring a beer in Italy, 1949. Lucky was just released by police in Rome after being questioned regarding a drug ring. He was ordered to stay out of the city.

The system worked well and the Syndicate prospered. Each crime family went about their various rackets, and relative harmony was kept, partly through the Syndicate enforcement arm, dubbed Murder, Inc. Under Luciano's leadership, organized crime made a fortune during Prohibition, and after Repeal continued to rake in millions with narcotics trafficking, gambling, and prostitution. It was this last racket that ended Luciano's luck. In 1936, the tenacious New York District Attorney, Thomas E. Dewey, had set his sights on Luciano (and on attaining the Governor's office), and built up a damning case against the mobster that eventually sent him away for a perhaps cruel and unusual thirty to fifty-year sentence for prostitution. Charles Luciano was sent as far away from New York City as the state borders would allow, to Clinton State Prison near Canada, to serve out his time, and possibly the rest of his life.

December 7, 1941, brought World War II to American shores, and along

with it, German U-Boats that began attacking and sinking ships in U.S. shipping lanes. The USS *Normandie*, an ocean liner being renovated as a troop ship, burned and capsized off a Manhattan pier. Sabotage was suspected. The United States Navy decided that, in order to prevent further incidents, it needed to employ the help of fishermen and dockworkers in and around the various ports of New York City and Long Island. But the fishing industry and the docks were controlled by the mob, and the mob wasn't cooperating. The Navy contacted Meyer Lansky, who told them that the only person who could help them was sitting in a prison near the Canadian border.

At Lansky's request, the Navy had Luciano moved to a prison closer to New York City, near Albany. From there Lansky and various members of the Syndicate paid Charlie Lucky many visits over the following months. Luciano instructed the boss of the Fulton Fish Market, Joseph "Socks" Lanza, to cooperate with the Navy. When all was said and done, it was the mob that supplied crucial information that foiled a plot involving well-financed German saboteurs entering the United States via U-Boats, with plans to attack American

Right: January 9, 1946: Luciano (right), handcuffed to unidentified guard, being transported to Sing Sing prison in preparation for his deportation to Italy.

targets from within. In 1946, Lucky Luciano, for his contribution to the war effort, was granted a parole from prison, but having never received American citizenship, was deported to his native Italy.

Luciano tried to stay active in the American Syndicate from Italy, but it wasn't easy. In 1946 Lucky traveled to Cuba, and called a meeting of the Commission and announced his plans to run his crime family from Havana until he could find a way to return to the United States legally. (It was also supposedly at this meeting that Bugsy Siegel was given his death sentence.) But the Justice Department got wind of the plans and lobbied the Cuban government to expel Luciano back to Italy. The Cubans bowed to U.S. pressure and soon sent Charlie Lucky packing.

Luciano stayed marginally involved in the Syndicate, trying to run his family through Joe Adonis and Frank Costello, and aiding in a plot to bring down the ambitious Vito Genovese. There are also stories of his involvement in an Italian narcotics trade that

blossomed into an international crime syndicate. Luciano was reportedly under suspicion of heroin trafficking when he collapsed in the Naples airport on January 26, 1962, and died of a massive heart attack. Finally allowed to return to the country from which he was exiled, Lucky was buried in Queens, New York, in a crypt inscribed with his given name *Lucania*. The inscription reads, "*Il Nostro Caro Fratello*," Our Beloved Brother.

Above: Luciano called a press conference in Rome in 1948 to "set the record straight." He is seen here enjoying a drink with reporters at the Excelsior Hotel.

Left: Homecoming: Luciano's body is interred in the family mausoleum in St. Johns Cemetery in Queens on February 8, 1962.

October 25, 1957:
Albert Anastasia
murdered

November 4, 1957:
Apalachin
Conference raid

June 6, 1962:
Joe Profaci dies

May 2, 1957:
Frank Costello
shot, retires as
head of crime family

February 25, 1957:
Bugs Moran dies
in prison

January 6, 1962:
Lucky Luciano
dies in Italy

April 24, 1965:
Owney Madden
dies

June 28, 1971:
Joe Colombo sh
dies seven years

November 26, 1
Joe Adonis dies
in Italy

February 27, 1959:
Abner Zwillman
dead of apparent
suicide

July 13, 1967:
Tommy
Lucchese
dies

April 1951:
Vincent Mangano
missing, presumed
dead

February 14, 1969:
Vito Genovese
dies in prison

1950

1960

1970

Brave New Mob

The End of an Era

April 7, 1972:
Joey Gallo murdered
in Little Italy

January 15, 1983:
Meyer Lansky
dies

May 11, 2002:
Joe Bonanno
dies at age 97

February 18, 1973:
Frank Costello dies

June 19, 1975:
Sam Giancana
found murdered

October 15, 1976:
Carlo Gambino
dies

1976:
Mickey
Cohen dies

July 11, 1984:
Raymond Patriarca
dies

1989:
Moe Dalitz dies

1980   **1990**   **2000**

Brave New Mob
The End of an Era

The Kefauver Committee hearings of the early 1950s brought the problem of organized crime in America to a national audience. It marked the beginning of a new era for mobsters that saw a renewed commitment by government and police officials to root out organized crime throughout the country. In a way, it also marked the beginning of the end of the mob's golden age.

In 1957, police raided a house in Apalachin, New York, finding a gathering of America's mob kingpins. The exposure of that meeting again highlighted the prevalence of organized crime in the country and forced FBI director J. Edgar Hoover to launch a program that targeted top mobsters. This was a further erosion of Hoover's official stance that organized crime did not even exist in America. In 1963, Joseph Valachi's insider testimony gave a new name to organized crime, *La Cosa Nostra*, which finally shattered any remaining arguments against a nationally organized crime syndicate.

Yet despite all the high profile media attention and legal scrutiny, by the end of the 1950s and into the 1960s, the role of organized crime in American and world politics began to take on new dimensions. The govern-

ment had made use of mob intelligence going back to World War II, when Lucky Luciano was released from prison for information relating to German sabotage plans on the New York waterfront. But in the 1960s, the relationship between organized crime and the U.S. government took an unexpected turn when the CIA reportedly took out a mob hit on Fidel Castro. Since that time there have been allegations that the mob has been involved in clandestine government and CIA activities, including various assassinations, up to and including a United States president. This was a brave new world and an even braver new mob.

Opposite: Chicago mobster Sam Giancana was part of a new generation of mobsters.

Below: Joseph Valachi (seated extreme right) testifying before a Senate committee. Seen at rear are charts of New York's crime families as identified by Valachi.

Sam Giancana

"Giancana should be considered armed and dangerous since he allegedly has a vicious temperament, phychopatic [sic] personality and has been known to carry firearms."

—1960 FBI REPORT

A boy is born to a poor family and turns to crime in order to make money. He joins a gang and works his way up through the ranks, gaining more power until eventually he is the boss of a crime family. When in his later years his presence is seen as a threat to the general health of the mob, he is taken out. The story could belong to any number of mobsters. But then add to the mix the 42ers, the CIA, Operation Mongoose, the Outfit, Marilyn Monroe and the Kennedy clan, and a host of Hollywood stars and starlets, and the story becomes unmistakably that of Sam "Mooney" Giancana. Murder, sex, money, king making, international intrigue, assassinations; the stories often sound like a who's who of conspiracy theories. In the 1960s, Sam Giancana truly was a brave new mobster.

Momo Salvatore Giancana was born on June 15, 1908, in a mostly Italian Chicago ghetto known as the Patch. With a father who was given to violence, and little hope of escape from poverty, Sam left school after the sixth grade and began hanging out with a group of young toughs known as the 42 Gang. The 42ers were young, dangerous, and hungry. For many, the gang was a place to hone their skills at robbery, racketeering, and murder before graduating to the big leagues of the mob.

Sam Giancana was called up to the mob's major league by bosses Anthony "Big Tuna" Accardo and Paul "the Waiter" Ricca. Giancana worked for the Chicago Outfit as a wheelman, personal chauffeur for the powerful mobsters, and hired gun. One story from Mooney's brother, Chuck Giancana, in his book *Double Cross,* reportedly compiled from recollections of conversations with the mobster over five decades, claims that Mooney had been called up earlier by Al Capone to help in his quest to own Chicago. The story goes that it was Capone who plotted to take out his boss and friend, Johnny Torrio, and not the O'Banion gang seeking revenge for the murder of their boss, as is generally believed. The plot was carried out, but Torrio narrowly survived. He retired anyway, leaving the boss spot to Capone. Chuck Giancana tells of the lead gunner in the Torrio hit being none other than Sam Giancana. It seems unlikely, however, that if it was Capone who ordered the hit on Torrio, that he would trust an untried, un-made seventeen-year-old thug to do a deed with such dire consequences should the attempt end in failure.

Opposite: Sam Giancana in 1965. His mild-mannered appearance belied a vicious nature.

Above: Mod mobster: Sam Giancana walking in downtown Chicago in 1965.

In 1929, Giancana was sent to prison for three years on a burglary conviction. When he emerged from Joliet Prison in 1932, the criminal landscape had changed. Prohibition was coming to an end and Capone had been sent to prison for tax evasion. In his place he appointed Ricca and Accardo to run the Outfit, which thrived in relative post-Capone peace, extending its reach far beyond the Windy City. Giancana also thrived, continuing his rise in the Outfit and supplying post-Prohibition rotgut at cut-rate prices. However, it was this activity that bought him a four-year trip to Leavenworth in 1939.

Four years in prison can never be a good thing, but as it happened, this particular stint in the joint was to help promote Mooney Giancana to head of the Chicago Outfit. While serving out his sentence, Sam came into contact with black Chicago policy banker Eddie Jones. Jones told Giancana about the wheel rackets in the city, which had made him a multimillionaire with property and holdings throughout the world. The rackets were similar to other numbers games around the country where small bets and modest payouts led to enormous profits for those running the banks. Armed with the knowledge from Jones, Giancana returned to the streets of Chicago in 1943 with a plan to take over the policy rackets.

Mooney's plan was simple and time-tested: intimidate and kill. Upon Jones' release from prison, Giancana repaid him for the policy lesson by kidnapping him for ransom. After holding the policy banker for a week, Jones was finally released for $100,000 plus all of his policy rackets and equipment. Giancana continued in the following years on his campaign to rule the policy rackets of Chicago. One policy banker who stood in his way was Teddy Roe. Roe wouldn't go out as easily as Jones, however, and ended up in retirement permanently, shot down in the street after a prolonged war with the Outfit.

By the 1950s the money that the policy rackets provided the Outfit was substantial, and earned Sam Giancana considerable respect from Ricca and Accardo, who went into a sort of semi-retirement to avoid legal troubles. Giancana was promoted to boss, although Ricca and Accardo appear to have had final say in all business matters. The Outfit had been extending both its political and business reach, buying politicians and elections, and moving into gambling, with a nationwide race wire service, as well as interests in casinos in Las Vegas and Cuba. Giancana claimed to own many politicians and government officials along the way, including Bobby and Jack Kennedy. It's often reported that

Joe Kennedy owed the mob for many favors, including when Mooney, through various means, delivered pivotal Illinois votes to JFK during the 1960 election, which won the presidency for Kennedy in one of the closest races in U.S. history. But if the story were true, why would Bobby Kennedy, as newly appointed United States Attorney General, so doggedly pursue organized crime? Mooney's answer was that both JFK and Bobby Kennedy were purposely trying to cover the tracks of their checkered family involvement with the mob and were engaged in a desperate attempt to rewrite Kennedy family history. For turning their backs on the mob, both Kennedys paid the ultimate price.

Here, many stories about Sam Giancana's contributions to history begin to push the boundaries of believability. One story tells of Giancana's sexual relationship with and eventual murder of Marilyn Monroe, officially ruled a suicide, in order to frame and humiliate the Kennedys. Another theory has been put forth that Giancana was involved in the assassinations of both JFK and Bobby Kennedy as payback for their betrayal, as well as the silencing of Lee Harvey Oswald for his CIA/mob connections. And in fact, there have been links found between Giancana and Oswald's killer, Jack Ruby. Then there is the murky relationship between Mooney and the CIA itself. It is generally acknowledged that the CIA employed Giancana and other mobsters to put a hit on communist Cuban leader Fidel Castro, in a plot codenamed Operation Mongoose. Regardless of which stories are true and which are fabricated or exaggerated, they illustrate a time of turmoil and change in the American psyche in which the lines of good and evil began to blur and grand conspiracies, previously ignored, could begin to be seen as plausible.

The last years of Sam Giancana's life were spent under constant surveillance by the CIA and FBI, and dogged pursuit by the Justice Department. Giancana fled to Mexico in the late 1960s to avoid prosecution, living a life of luxurious semi-retirement. But pressure on the Mexican government led to Mooney's extradition back to the United States in 1974. In failing health and advancing age he was scheduled to testify to a Senate committee on his role in the Outfit and relationship to the CIA. To many in the mob and in the government, Giancana had become a liability.

On June 19, 1975, Sam Giancana was found dead in the basement kitchen of his Oak Park, Illinois, home. Police saw no sign of forced entry or struggle, only an old man who had been cooking sausages when someone put a bullet in the back of his head. To make sure he was dead, five more bullets were fired under his chin and through his mouth into his brain. Whatever his deeds, whatever his secrets, whatever his sins, Sam Giancana's killer made sure that Momo would not live to reveal them.

VITAL SIGNS

Born: June 15, 1908
Died: June 19, 1975
Cause of Death: Murdered (shot)
Buried: Mount Carmel Cemetery; Hillside, Illinois

SCREEN TIME

Sugartime (1995) (TV). Played by John Turturro
Sinatra (1992) (TV). Played by Rod Steiger
Mafia Princess (1986) (TV). Played by Tony Curtis

Raymond Patriarca

"…in this thing of ours, your love for your mother and father is one thing, your love for The Family is a different kind of love.

—RAYMOND PATRIARCA IN FBI SURVEILLANCE TAPE

For those Raymond Patriarca considered friends, he'd live up to his nickname, *El Padrone,* The Patriarch. He took care of his New England crime family as if they were his own flesh and blood. He was not as hospitable to those he considered enemies or to those who endangered the family. Ray Patriarca once reportedly put out a hit on his own brother for not detecting an FBI bug. In the end he didn't have his brother killed, but he had made his point. No one would stand in his way.

Raymond Loreda Salvatore Patriarca was born in Worcester, Massachusetts, in 1908. His family relocated to Providence, Rhode Island, three years later where his father operated a liquor store. There is no record of any criminal activity by Patriarca until his father's death in 1925. At the age of seventeen Patriarca was arrested on violation of Prohibition laws in Connecticut. This was the beginning of a string of arrests (twenty-eight in all) that would span the rest of his life. Charges included murder, conspiracy to commit murder, white slavery, armed robbery, breaking and entering, and prison escape.

In 1938, Patriarca was arrested and convicted for his role in an armed robbery of a Massachusetts jewelry store. He was sentenced to three to five years, but with friends in high places, he served only a few months. A government corruption investigation followed that led all the way to the governor's office. Upon his release from prison, Patriarca set about building his power in Providence.

A two-story building on Atwells Avenue in the Federal Hill area housed his front businesses, National Cigarette Service Company and Coin-O-Matic Distributors, in addition to being the headquarters of his crime network. Patriarca's only rival in Providence was an Irishman, Carlton O'Brien, who controlled most of the gambling and loansharking rackets in the area. One method of gaining market share is to eliminate the competition. Patriarca did just that by having his men shoot O'Brien to death in 1952. Having sole control over Providence, it wasn't long before Patriarca exercised control over all of New England.

In 1954, Filippo Buccola retired from heading the Boston crime family and named Patriarca as his successor. This marked the beginning of Providence as the base of power for the New England crime family that would last for decades. The territory stretched from the Connecticut River into Maine. But Patriarca had influence well beyond New England. He

Opposite:
Raymond Patriarca smokes a cigarette in Providence, Rhode Island, in this undated photo.

that narcotics dealing crossed a moral boundary and no self-respecting Mafioso would deal in them. Other accounts tell of a system where freelance drug dealers were allowed to operate for a fee.

But drug dealing or no, the New England crime family thrived for decades under Patriarca, who commanded loyalty and respect among both mobsters and street thugs with a combination of ruthlessness and beneficence. Those who served him loyally were well compensated. Those who crossed him were dealt with harshly. In total, Patriarca spent six years in prison for conspiracy to commit murder, including his role in the shotgun murders of four mobsters. It was the testimony of snitch Joseph "the Animal" Barboza that helped put Patriarca away. In 1967, Barboza, a hitman for Patriarca, was considered the Joe Valachi of the New England crime family. His testimony helped, among other things, to put four men on death row. Recently released FBI files show, however, that Barboza may have been lying to save his own skin, and in fact framed some members of the mob for crimes that Barboza himself had committed. (The files also show that the FBI was well aware of this fact and prosecuted the men anyway.) For his role in testifying against the mob, Barboza was murdered in San Francisco by unknown assailants in 1976.

Above: Patriarca was identified by the Boston D.A. to testify before the traveling Kefauver Committee in 1950, but the hearings never ended up in Boston.

built connections with New York's crime families, including the Profaci and Genovese families, and his underboss, Henry Tameleo had been a member of the Bonanno crime family. He had deals in Las Vegas casinos and various rackets in Philadelphia and Florida, which included gambling, prostitution, loansharking, and drug trafficking, although accounts vary on this last item. One account holds that Patriarca was of the old-school mind

---

VITAL SIGNS

Born: 1908
Died: July 11, 1984
Cause of Death: Natural causes (heart attack)
Buried: Gates of Heaven Cemetery; East Providence, Rhode Island

While serving his sentence, Patriarca continued to run his New England crime family from behind bars. But Barboza had done permanent damage to Patriarca. He was behind bars from 1969 until 1975 for murder conspiracy convictions. Various arrests followed throughout his final years for past deeds, including a charge in 1978 by snitch Vincent Teresa, that Patriarca played a role in the CIA plot to kill Cuban leader Fidel Castro. Teresa claimed that the CIA took out a contract with the mob on Castro and that Patriarca helped select the hitman. On July 11, 1984, Patriarca was rushed to the hospital in cardiac arrest, where he soon died at the age of 76. Even at that advanced age, El Padrone was under indictment for two murders.

Above: Joseph "the Animal" Barboza is sworn in before testifying for the House Crime Committee in 1972. Barboza was an informant for the FBI, which overlooked his many serious crimes in exchange for information and testimony.

Left: "El Padrone" in cuffs in 1967 is led to court by an FBI agent. He was being tried for conspiracy to commit murder.

Joe Profaci

"Even if we go hijack some trucks, [Profaci] taxes us. I paid up to $1,800."

—CARMINE "THE SNAKE" PERSICO AS QUOTED BY JOSEPH VALACHI

By the time of his death in 1962, Joseph Profaci was one of only two New York bosses still in control of their crime families since the time of the Castellammarese War. His longevity as a mob boss was impressive, and in its own way, admirable. Thirty-two years is a long time to survive at the top of any business, especially considering that many who served under Profaci were actively trying to kill him.

Joe Profaci was born in Sicily on October 2, 1897. He arrived in New York in 1922 and soon began his life-long career in crime. Unlike many young thugs who got their foot in the door as muscle and hired guns for older, more established mobsters, Profaci seemed to set out on his own building his criminal empire. By the time the Castellammarese War was settled in 1931 with the murders of Joe Masseria and Salvatore Maranzano, Profaci was powerful enough to be admitted into the newly formed Syndicate as head of his own crime family, one of five in New York City.

Throughout the 1930s, Profaci expanded into many illegal enterprises, including loansharking, narcotics trafficking, and prostitution, as well as many legitimate businesses. He was, at one time, considered the largest importer of olive oil and tomato paste in America. He owned businesses that dealt in alcohol sales and distribution, linen supply, real estate, and held interests in the garment industry. Combined with his illegal enterprises, Profaci's income was impressive. He owned a 328-acre estate in New Jersey that reportedly included several large, heavily secured houses, a hunting lodge, and a private airstrip.

Yet despite his substantial personal wealth, some of Profaci's management techniques were seen as greedy and even petty and earned him the loathing of many who served under him. One often repeated example concerns a $25 monthly fee that Profaci would charge each of his men. A common practice of early gang leaders, the collected dues would be placed in a fund that would go towards legal defense fees and graft money. The practice had long since been abandoned by most mob bosses who viewed it as an outmoded form of tribute. In addition, Profaci also collected a sort of tax from anyone doing criminal activities in his territory, demanding a significant, disproportionate cut of any and every job done within his borders. Such practices were not unusual among mob bosses, but Profaci was known for his brutal enforcement of his high and non-negotiable tariffs.

One legendary Profaci story concerns a crown stolen from a Brooklyn

Opposite: Joe Profaci testifying before the Senate Rackets Committee in 1958. Profaci stated his name and address, then invoked his Fifth Amendment rights against self-incrimination.

Above: Profaci (left) with his underboss Joseph Magliocco in federal court in 1959. The two were facing conspiracy charges in connection with the 1957 mob meeting in Apalachin, New York.

Opposite, bottom: Profaci's mausoleum in St. Johns Cemetery in Queens, New York.

Opposite, top: Carmine Persico in 1963.

church. Reportedly a devout Catholic, Profaci put out word that the crown was to be returned or a death sentence would be ordered for the thief. The crown was promptly

---

VITAL SIGNS

Born: October 2, 1897 (dates vary)
Died: June 6, 1962
Cause of Death: Natural causes (cancer)
Buried: St. Johns Cemetery; Queens, New York

SCREEN TIME

Bonanno: A Godfather's Story (1999) (TV). Played by Silvio Oliviero
Love, Honor & Obey: The Last Mafia Marriage (1993) (TV). Played by Tomas Milian
Mobsters (1991). Played by Joe Viterelli

---

returned, but the burgular was killed anyway, strangled to death with a rosary. The murder would serve as a lesson to all those who would dare to cross Joe Profaci.

The case of Frankie Shots Abbatemarco exemplifies Profaci's crass management style. The Brooklyn policy banker had the audacity to balk at a $50,000 tribute payment Profaci demanded in order to do business in his territory. Profaci ordered a hit on Frankie Shots, and contracted the job out to Larry and "Crazy Joey" Gallo, two family lieutenants who have long been connected with the slaying of mob boss, Albert Anastasia. In exchange for the hit, Profaci reportedly promised the Gallos a portion of Abbatemarco's rackets. The Gallos agreed and lived up to their end of the deal by whacking Abbatemarco. Profaci, however, developed a case of amnesia and forgot all about the deal, instead parceling out Frankie Shots' rackets to his family and friends.

The Gallos joined a growing faction of Profaci mob members who were disgruntled with their boss's miserly ways. A small war broke out that included several kidnappings and killings. Eventually Profaci managed to divide his enemies against one another, but had to continue fending off the Gallos until his death.

Despite his murderous, iron-fisted rule, Profaci apparently saw no irony in his devout Catholic beliefs. The Profaci home was said to have had a private altar for mass at family gatherings. And a petition was made to Pope Pius XII in Rome to bestow a churchly knighthood on Profaci. The petition failed when the Brooklyn district attorney took it upon himself to write a letter disabusing the Pope of any notion that the saintly Joe Profaci was anything but a murderous, thieving American mob boss.

Joe Profaci died of cancer on June 6, 1962, still heading his crime family until the very end. After thirty-two years as one of America's most powerful and notorious mob bosses, Profaci narrowly missed having his name permanently tied to his crime family. In 1963, mob informer Joe Valachi named Profaci's successor, Joeseph Magliocco, as one of the bosses of New York's five crime families (the crime family's name was soon changed to that of one of his successors, Joe Colombo). Had he lived to hear Valachi sing, Profaci might have made the cut and kept the family name in the family business.

"The Snake"

The group of rebels that had reportedly joined forces against their former boss, Joe Profaci, included Carmine "the Snake" Persico who had a reputation as a vicious enforcer. There is plenty of mob lore surrounding Persico. One story tells of the Snake getting shot in the face by rival mobsters while sitting in a car. For some reason the bullet remained in his mouth. The Snake spat the bullet out and drove himself to the hospital. Another story has it that Profaci split the rebel faction that warred against him by offering Persico a sort of amnesty if he took out the Gallos. Persico reportedly invited Larry Gallo to a restaurant for a conference, then threw a rope around his neck and began strangling him. Gallo's life was narrowly spared when a cop happened to walk into the restaurant at just that moment. The incident was later to be portrayed in *The Godfather: Part II*.

OFFICIAL CALENDAR   LEWIS J. VALENTINE.

POLICE DEPARTMENT
CITY OF NEW YORK

SATURDAY
2
JUNE
1945

40201

Vito Genovese

"If you went to him and told him about some guy doing wrong he would have the guy killed, and then he would have you killed for telling on the guy."

—MOB INFORMANT JOSEPH VALACHI, ON VITO GENOVESE

The case can be made that Vito Genovese was inadvertently responsible for many things now known about the mob, including its rituals, codes, history, and even the names still used to identify most of New York's five crime families. This information, and plenty more, was provided by mob informer Joe Valachi, who flipped for the Feds in order to gain protection from the man he believed was trying to kill him, the man known to many as "Don Vito."

Born on November 24, 1897, Vito Genovese spent the first fifteen years of his life in Risigliano, a town near Naples, Italy. His family moved to New York in 1913, where his father operated a small contracting business. The teenage Vito did not take long to figure out where the big money was to be made. Ever the opportunist, Genovese began running with street gangs on Manhattan's Lower East Side. At this time Genovese met a young Charlie "Lucky" Luciano. The two were allied in their ambitions to take over the underworld from their older, shortsighted bosses. But despite their shared goals, they also had a mutual distrust of one another. As Luciano would later recount, "I had a feeling in my bones that someday Vito was going to be bad news for everybody."

Making a name for himself as a competent gunman and muscle, Genovese was arrested over a dozen times for assault, robbery and murder, once serving sixty days for carrying a gun, but otherwise evading conviction. Genovese is widely believed to be one of the gunmen who killed Joe the Boss Masseria in a Coney Island restaurant in 1931.

Vito Genovese's life story often sounds like a soap opera. At times, his FBI files read like so much gossip. His first wife died in 1931, and Vito soon began courting another woman, who was married at the time. Genovese made her a widow in 1932 when he killed her husband, only to wed her himself twelve days later. His best man at the wedding was Anthony Strollo, also known as Tony Bender, whom Don Vito would also eventually have killed. In 1953 his wife (who was reportedly having a lesbian affair with a waitress in one of Genovese's clubs), filed for divorce and spilled the beans in court about his illegal activities. She also claimed that Genovese wanted to marry the wife of one of his henchmen, a man whose daughter was married to Vito's son. But all that came later.

In 1937, in an effort to avoid being charged for a murder committed three years earlier, Genovese fled the United States and returned to his native Italy. It was there that Genovese reportedly

Opposite: 1945 New York Police Department mug shot of Vito Genovese following his return to the U.S. from Italy to face murder charges. Genovese was acquitted after the witness in the case was found dead in police custody.

Right: Genovese waiting to appear before a Trenton, New Jersey, grand jury in 1957. The grand jury was investigating Genovese's attendance of the mob conference in Apalachin, New York. In his ten-minute testimony, Genovese invoked the Fifth Amendment fifty times.

allied himself with Benito Mussolini, despite the fascist dictator's campaign to eradicate the Mafia in Italy. But towards the end of World War II, when the Allies invaded and occupied Italy, Genovese easily switched sides again and began working for the United States Army as a translator. Before long, however, it was discovered that the translator was at the head of an operation that was stealing American supplies and selling them on the black market. When Army officials learned that Genovese was wanted back in the U.S. for murder, he was returned to face trial, only to find that the witness against him had died in protective custody after having been given enough poison "to kill eight horses."

There had been some changes in the underworld in Genovese's absence. Lucky Luciano had been deported to Italy and Frank Costello was sitting in as acting head of his crime family. Lucky's thwarted attempt to run his family from Cuba until he could find a way to get back to America may have been more than just the workings of the Justice Department. Luciano would later say that he suspected that

the tip-off to the United States government came from Vito Genovese.

Genovese was never one to sit back peacefully and go about his business. Having helped to marginalize Luciano, he next set his sights on becoming not only the boss of his crime family, but also the head of the Syndicate, as *capo di tutti capi*. To do so would require a reorganization of the Commission in his favor. In his way stood Frank Costello and Albert Anastasia.

After Vincent "the Chin" Gigante took a shot at Costello in 1957, Costello abdicated his position as boss. Next up was Albert Anastasia. Genovese reportedly persuaded Anastasia's underboss, Carlo Gambino, to knock off his boss. In exchange, Vito would ensure that Gambino would take Anastasia's spot as head of his family. The assumption was that Don Vito would have Gambino's loyalty, thus further shoring up his power. Gambino's men did a better job of it than "the Chin" and offed Anastasia in a barber chair. With all impediments removed from his ascendancy to the throne, a meeting of the mob bosses was called that would likely crown Don Vito the king of the underworld.

── VITAL SIGNS ──

Born: November 24, 1897
Died: February 14, 1969
Cause of Death: Natural causes
Buried: St. Johns Cemetery; Queens, New York

── SCREEN TIME ──

Boss of Bosses (2001) (**TV**). Played by Steven Bauer (with Chazz Palminteri as Paul Castellano)
The Valachi Papers (1972). Played by Lino Ventura (with Charles Bronson as Joe Valachi)

But the crowning was not to be. State police raided the Apalachin, New York, estate of Joseph Barbara and found an extraordinary gathering that comprised a veritable who's who of America's Mob kingpins. Many of the men at the gathering escaped into the surrounding woods, but most, including Vito Genovese, were arrested and taken in for questioning. A search of their personal belongings yielded, among other things, some $300,000 in cash between them. Every man detained repeated the same story, that they were merely visiting an ailing Joseph Barbara, coincidentally on the exact same day.

The Apalachin fiasco had far-reaching consequences. Vito Genovese was not crowned as head of the mob, but rather was widely blamed among mobsters for the humiliating episode. FBI director, J. Edgar Hoover, who had previously denied the very existence of an American Mafia, began a high-profile investigation into organized crime less than two weeks after the incident. There could no longer be any doubt that there did exist in America a very organized, very extensive, very powerful national crime syndicate. And there has also been the suggestion that the raid at Apalachin was part of an elaborate setup to bring down the man who would be king.

Just six months after Apalachin, Vito Genovese was arrested and convicted of narcotics trafficking and sent to prison on a fifteen-year sentence. It was later revealed by Luciano that the drug rap had been part of the plan to set up Genovese for a big fall. Don Vito had misread Carlo Gambino, who along with Luciano, Lansky and Costello, conspired to frame Genovese by providing evidence to the government that would send Genovese to prison for what eventually amounted to a life sentence.

While in federal prison in Atlanta, Georgia, Genovese continued to run his crime family through his brother, Michael. It was there that Don Vito came into close contact with a low-level Genovese soldier named Joseph Valachi. Over time, an increasingly paranoid Genovese came to wrongly believe that Valachi was an informant, and delivered to him the fabled "kiss of death." A duly terrified Valachi, in order to save his own skin, decided to become exactly what Genovese suspected him to be. His resulting testimony before a Senate subcommittee yielded volumes of information concerning the workings of the Syndicate and gave name to New York's five crime families.

While his crime family still bears his name to this day, Vito Genovese was never able to fully realize his own aspirations. In 1969, Genovese died in prison of natural causes. Driven by the desire for power, Genovese was ultimately brought down by his own raw ambition. His legacy may very well be the knowledge gained concerning the workings of the underworld that Don Vito sought to own.

"Our Thing"

Another interesting bit of information from Valachi was the term *cosa nostra*, literally translated as "our thing." This is the term that Valachi used to describe the organization to which he belonged. According to Valachi, terms like *Mafia* were used by the media and outsiders, but never by wiseguys. Subsequently, the fictional proper name *La Cosa Nostra*, or LCN, became the preferred term to many when describing the mob, and allowed J. Edgar Hoover some political cover. In an attempt to deflect criticism after Valachi's testimony, Hoover, having virtually ignored organized crime for over quarter of a century, reported to the media that the FBI had known about LCN for years.

Above: Joseph Valachi testifying before the Senate Permanent Investigation Committee. Valachi demonstrates the mob ritual of initiation in which a crumpled piece of paper was burned in his hand while reciting the oath to "live by the gun and the knife and to die by the gun and the knife" and to be burned to ashes if he should ever betray their trust.

Joey Gallo

*"He made a mistake, Crazy Joe did.
He should have gone to bed last night."*
—New York Deputy Police Commissioner Robert Daley to a
reporter at the scene of Gallo's murder

In 1975, Bob Dylan wrote a song about a misunderstood young man who was persecuted by the law. Dylan never knew Joey Gallo, but Jacques Levy, who co-wrote the song "Joey" did know the mobster and told his story to Dylan, who was captivated by the tale. The story of "Crazy Joe" Gallo also caught the attention of Jimmy Breslin, whose novel, *The Gang That Couldn't Shoot Straight*, was supposedly closely modeled after the Gallo gang. The novel was later made into a film of the same name. However, Breslin's depiction of the mobster, as the title might indicate, wasn't quite as flattering as Dylan's version. Regardless of which version is correct, Joey Gallo was a fascinating figure in mob history.

Joseph Gallo was born in 1929 in Red Hook, Brooklyn. He and his two brothers, Larry and Albert "Kid Blast" Gallo, began an early life of crime, with Joey's first arrest at age seventeen for assault, kidnapping, and burglary. At first the Gallos were only loosely affiliated with the mob. However, one disputed story tells of Joey Gallo being made into the Profaci crime family for carrying out a contract on infamous mob boss Albert Anastasia, who was shot down in a hotel barbershop. After

Anastasia's murder, Gallo, referring to himself and four of his associates, was said to brag, "From now on you can call us the barbershop quintet." Gallo was questioned by police concerning the murder, but was never charged.

Life in the Profaci family was no picnic. Joseph Profaci ruled his organization with an iron fist, with death sentences for insubordination, and excessive taxes and tributes due to Profaci from each man under his authority and operating in his territory. In short, Profaci may have inspired fear within his ranks, but he did not inspire loyalty. The Gallos discovered this when they carried out a

Opposite: Joey Gallo smokes a cigarette while waiting to appear in a Brooklyn court in 1961.

Left: "Crazy Joey" Gallo in 1961.

Right: The
Brothers Gallo:
Joey (in tie) and
Larry are escorted
by unidentified
man between them
in 1961.

hit on policy banker, "Frankie Shots" Abbatemarco, at the behest of Profaci for failure to deliver tribute. In return for the hit, the Gallos were promised a portion of Abbatemarco's rackets. After the contract was carried out, however, Profaci conveniently forgot his promise. The Gallos, along with other disgruntled crime family members, angrily broke away from Profaci and declared war on their former don.

The war continued for years, costing many lives from both sides. It continued even after Profaci died of cancer in 1962, and was passed on to one of his successors, Joe Colombo, who would become a victim of the war himself (although Carlo Gambino may have had a hand in it as well). On June 28, 1971, Colombo was shot in the head at an Italian unity rally that he had organized. The shooting left Colombo alive but in a vegetative state until his eventual death seven years later. It is widely believed that the shooter, a lone black man who was killed by Colombo's bodyguards, was probably acting under the orders of Joey Gallo.

But for much of the duration of the Gallo-Profaci dispute, Joey Gallo was behind bars. He was sent to prison in January 1962 on an extortion rap, and wasn't released until March of 1971. It was during his time in prison that Gallo underwent a sort of renaissance.

Crazy Joe, looking at a long stretch in prison, decided that instead of twiddling his thumbs, he would set about educating himself. He reportedly read two newspapers a day as well as classic literature and philosophy. He also took up painting. And unlike other Italian Mafiosi, Gallo also became friends with black inmates. In addition to harboring relatively little racial animosity, Gallo also knew that having good relations with black mobsters would be an asset, as black gangs were becoming more and more prominent and powerful in New York.

Joey Gallo emerged from prison in 1971 a more educated and refined man, if not a reformed one.

At about the time of his release, there was another release that would have an impact on Gallo's life. The film version of *The Gang That Couldn't Shoot Straight* came out in 1971. It was a comic tale of hapless mobsters, reportedly modeled on the Gallos, right down to the pet lion the Gallos reportedly kept in a Brooklyn basement as an incentive for payment on delinquent loans. Despite an understandably negative review of the film on the Gallos' part, Joey sought out actor Jerry Orbach, who had played the role modeled after him. The two became friends and soon Joey Gallo was a regular at Broadway theaters and restaurants, and parties frequented by celebrities.

Orbach and his wife were at Gallo's 43rd birthday party at the Copacabana in Manhattan. They didn't join the party when it continued on in the wee hours of April 7, 1972, to Little Italy in search of a late night meal. Gallo and his party, which included his wife, bodyguard, and several other friends, settled in at a table at Umberto's Clam House on Mulberry Street. Apparently, some of Joe Colombo's men had wit-

---

VITAL SIGNS

Born: April 6, 1929
Died: April 7, 1972
Cause of Death: Murdered (shot)
Buried: Green-Wood Cemetery; Brooklyn, New York

SCREEN TIME

Between Love & Honor (1995) (TV). Played by Michael Nouri
The Gang That Couldn't Shoot Straight (1971). Character "Kid Sally Palumbo" based on Gallo, played by Jerry Orbach

---

nessed the group enter the restaurant and saw their chance to revenge the shooting of their boss.

Some versions report that it was a single gunman who entered the restaurant and began firing, others say it was up to three. Regardless of the number, Joey Gallo's bodyguard, "Pete the Greek" Diapoulas, ended up with a bullet in his hip pocket. Gallo didn't fair as well. He managed to make it out onto Mulberry Street before he collapsed to the ground, dead.

Left: Umberto's Clam House in New York's Little Italy, where Joey Gallo was gunned down on April 7, 1972. His story inspired Bob Dylan to write the song "Joey."

Joe Colombo

"So the council had a meet about it, and one of the guys in Profaci's outfit named Joe Colombo come up with the idea of forming a legitimate association of Americans with Italian backgrounds to start a campaign against usin' just Italian names for them gangsters in the TV shows and movies."
—LUCKY LUCIANO ON THE FORMATION OF THE ITALIAN-AMERICAN CIVIL RIGHTS LEAGUE

Who was Joseph Colombo, Sr.? To many he was a hard-working businessman who crusaded against unfair treatment and depiction of Italian-Americans by the U.S. government and popular media. To others his campaigns for civil liberties were an ironic front to cover the fact that he was the boss of one of New York's five crime families. The truth is that Joe Colombo was all of these things.

Born in 1923, Joe was only fifteen years old when his father, Anthony, was murdered in what cops suspected to be a gangland hit. After a stint in the Coast Guard, where he was apparently granted a medical discharge for "psychoneurosis," Colombo began working on the New York waterfront as an enforcer and gambling organizer for the Profaci family. Colombo worked his way through the ranks in the crime family doing the bidding of his boss, including carrying out contract hits. One such contract would propel Joe Colombo to become the head of his own crime family.

After the death of Joe Profaci in 1962, Joe Magliocco was promoted as Profaci's successor. Another crime family head, Joe Bonanno decided to make a play to become the undisputed head of the mob by taking out Carlo Gambino, Tommy Lucchese, and several other mob bosses around the country. He approached Magliocco, who agreed not only to support the plan, but also to supply the assassins. His fateful choice was Joe Colombo. Some stories tell that Colombo had earlier, fond connections to the Gambino family. Others describe Colombo hearing opportunity knocking on his door. Whatever the reason, instead of carrying out the hit, Joe Colombo went to Gambino and told him of the plot. Gambino took that information to the Commission, where it was decided that Magliocco should retire. Bonanno refused to meet with the Commission and the ensuing battle was later referred to as the "Banana War." For his part, Joe Colombo was elevated to the position vacated by

Opposite: Joe Colombo displays a book of the history of the Italian-American Civil Rights League behind his desk at his real estate office in 1971.

Right: Joe Colombo, Sr., (in hood) and Joe, Jr., (far right) picketing at the FBI offices in Manhattan.

Magliocco. At forty years old, he was the youngest boss of a crime family that still retains his name to this day.

Immediately, Colombo put his stamp on the family by attempting to veil it with an air of legitimacy. He required all of the family's members to hold real jobs, in addition to their mob duties. Colombo himself held the job of real estate salesman. The real world jobs did not necessarily sit well with Colombo's men, however. After all, one of the perks of being a mobster is not having to collect garbage for a living. Whatever positive image may have been generated by the front, however, didn't fool the FBI. It was found that someone had taken Colombo's real estate certification test for him and forged his name.

As bizarre as Colombo's attempts at a legitimate front were, it was his founding of the Italian-American Civil Rights League that both created a mini social movement with Colombo as crusader and self-described hero, and also embarrassed the mob which in turn led to Colombo's eventual murder. It began, of all things, with members of Colombo's mob, including Joe himself, picketing the FBI headquarters

in Manhattan. The demonstration was an attempt to end the supposed harassment of Italian-Americans by the FBI and the Justice Department.

Spurred on by supporters, Colombo founded the IACRL, with the aim of improving the image of Italian-Americans in news and popular media, and also to deny the very existence of the American Mafia. The IACRL grew quickly and in a very short time managed to exercise influence over both media and government, branding the word "Mafia" as defamatory, and replacing it with the racially neutral "organized crime." The movement even managed to have all references to "Mafia" removed from a new movie that was being made called *The Godfather*, based on the best selling novel by Mario Puzo. In its short history, the IACRL managed to spawn many chapters across the country with membership in the thousands, hold political rallies, and bring in enormous amounts of cash. Some money was, no doubt, put into the causes espoused by the IACRL, but likely much of it went into Colombo's pockets.

The IACRL also held two rallies in Columbus Circle in Manhattan, the

---- VITAL SIGNS ----

Born: 1923
Died: May 22, 1978
Cause of Death: Murdered (shot on June 28, 1971, lived in vegetative state until death)
Buried: St. Johns Cemetery; Queens, New York

---- SCREEN TIME ----

Bonanno: A Godfather's Story (1999) (TV). Played by Domenic Deleo (with Edward James Olmos as Salvatore Maranzano)

site chosen in homage to the famous Italian explorer. The first rally, in 1970, was by all accounts a huge success. There was an enormous turnout with speeches by prominent politicians, entertainers, and the organizer himself, Joe Colombo, who billed himself as a prominent Italian-American businessman. "I say there is a conspiracy against me, against all Italian-Americans," he warned the crowd. "But you and I are together today, under God's eye, and those who get in our way will feel His sting."

The Syndicate, however, did not appreciate the attention generated by Joe Colombo's crusade. One key to success in the underworld is to remain, as the word itself suggests, *under*—under the radar of public outrage, police scrutiny, and resulting legal prosecution. Colombo's stirring the pot was causing multitudes of investigations to be launched against members of his crime family, and the Syndicate knew it was only a matter of time before those investigations were expanded to their own operations. Colombo was everybody's headache. He had to go.

The second IACRL rally, on June 28, 1971, was also its last. As the rally,

once again in Columbus Circle, was getting ready to begin, a black man stepped up to Joe Colombo and shot him in the head three times. The assassin, Jerome Johnson, was immediately shot to death by Colombo's men. Colombo, despite his massive wounds did not die, but instead went into a coma that lasted for the next seven years. He never regained consciousness and lived in a vegetative state until his death in 1978.

It is generally believed that Johnson was acting under the orders of "Crazy Joe" Gallo, who had a very old feud going with the Colombo Family stretching back to the days of Joe Profaci, and had friendly relations with many black criminals who would be willing to do just such a job. Gallo, in turn, was probably acting under the orders of Carlo Gambino and the Syndicate as a whole. With Joe Colombo in a permanent coma, the IACRL soon folded, and the status quo was restored. Organized crime was back in business as usual.

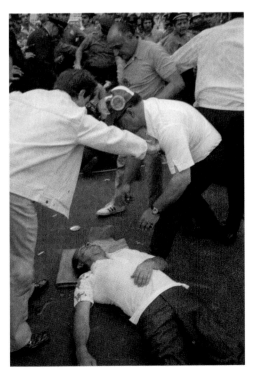

Left: Joe Colombo lies wounded just after being shot at an Italian-American unity rally in Columbus Circle in 1971. In the rear, police can be seen surrounding the mortally wounded Jerome Johnson.

Thomas Lucchese

"Tommy was no guy to owe money to."
—LUCKY LUCIANO

A story told by Lucky Luciano illustrates the nature of Tommy "Three-Finger Brown" Lucchese. A violin-playing bandleader, David Rubinoff, had borrowed $10,000 from Lucchese to buy an expensive Stradivarius. When Lucchese did not receive his payment, Luciano accompanied him to the club where the bandleader played to see if he could entice the musician to meet his financial obligations. In the back alley, Lucchese offered to bust a few of the musician's own fingers, ruining his livelihood, unless the money was paid back. The money was soon forthcoming, albeit borrowed from entertainer Eddie Cantor. Tommy Lucchese knew the power of subtle persuasion.

Gaetano Lucchese was born in Palermo, Sicily, in 1899 (the family spelled the name "Luckese," as is inscribed on the mobster's tombstone). Lucchese's family came to the United States about 1910 when Gaetano was just a small boy. He soon anglicized his name to Thomas, but always stayed small, reaching only 5'2" at his full height. Despite his small stature, Lucchese was bound for big things.

Tommy Lucchese always had a lot of irons in the fire. Running various rackets, from window cleaning to car theft, Tommy soon fell in with mobsters making big money in bootlegging. It was in Tom Reina's organi-zation in Harlem that Lucchese met Tom Gagliano. Gagliano would become Reina's successor and Lucchese would become his underboss when Reina became a casualty in the Castellammarese War. Little is known about the low-profile Gagliano, but he headed the crime family until he died in 1953. At that time Lucchese took over as boss of the organization that still bears his name today as one of New York's five crime families.

Opposite: 1952 New York police mug shot of Tommy Lucchese.

Below: "Three Finger Brown" is sworn in before testifying in front of the Senate Labor Rackets Committee.

none—not for lack of witnesses, but for lack of witnesses willing or able to testify. It was in the labor rackets, however, that Lucchese truly excelled. He was one of the first to exploit unions, which led to control of entire industries, with techniques that are still used today. One of the first industries under his thumb was the kosher chicken market in New York. By controlling the unions that trucked the specially prepared fowl to observant Jews, Lucchese was able to levy what amounted to a surcharge on every pound of chicken sold. But it was in the garment industry where Lucchese would really make his mark. Applying similar techniques of controlling the cartage, Tommy Lucchese was able to set prices and effectively control the garment industry in New York. Add to that his enormously effective and profitable loansharking business, in an industry that relies heavily on credit, and it wasn't long before Lucchese had personal ownership stakes in more than a dozen garment businesses in New York City.

With the wealth generated by his criminal activities, Tommy Lucchese was able to rack up an impressive list of personal friends in high places, including state and federal judiciary, New York police commissioners, district attorneys, and even congressmen. These friends helped him to become an American citizen in 1943, and more importantly kept him out of harm's way legally. Aside from an eighteen-month stint in his

Tommy Lucchese was into everything, including murder. Thirty killings have been credited to him personally and yet he was convicted of

---

━━━ SCREEN TIME ━━━

Love, Honor & Obey: The Last Mafia Marriage (1993) (TV). Played by Jerry Guarino (with Eric Roberts as Bill Bonanno)
The Gangster Chronicles (1981) (TV Miniseries). Played by Jon Polito (Narrated by E.G. Marshall)

━━━ VITAL SIGNS ━━━

Born: 1899
Died: July 13, 1967
Cause of Death: Natural causes (brain tumor)
Buried: Calvary Cemetery; Queens, New York

---

teenage years for boosting a car, Lucchese never spent any time in jail.

Lucchese also had a hand in drug trafficking. Mainly dealing in heroin, the business was an enormous source of revenue for the family. An incident involving the Lucchese family's drug trade was the apparent basis for the 1971 book and movie *The French Connection*, starring Gene Hackman and Roy Scheider.

Tommy Lucchese made his home in Lido Beach on Long Island, New York. His neighbors knew him as a businessman in the garment industry. He lived there in relative anonymity with his family. His son, Baldassare, was a graduate of West Point, but followed his father into the family business in the garment and labor rackets. His daughter, Frances, married the son of mob boss Carlo Gambino. The equivalent of a royal wedding, the union essentially joined the two mob families, if not in organization, at least in allegiance.

The Kefauver Committee hearings in the early 1950s essentially outed Lucchese as the leader of one of New York's five crime families. Although he avoided prosecution related to the hearings, he was forever tainted and labeled as a mobster. Upon his death on July 13, 1967, after battling with a brain tumor, Thomas Lucchese was laid to rest in Calvary Cemetery in Queens. Despite surveillance by police and the FBI, many underworld figures attended the ceremony, including Carlo Gambino, as a sign of respect.

Above: *Gene Hackman won best actor for his role as Popeye Doyle in the 1971 film* The French Connection, *based on an actual incident involving the Lucchese crime family.*

Above, right: *Chicago Cubs pitcher Mordecai Brown.*

"Three-Finger Brown"

The baseball player, Mordecai Brown, was a pitcher for the Chicago Cubs at the beginning of the 20th century. He gained a reputation as a fierce competitor and had a mean breaking ball that he could throw from spin generated by a stub where a finger used to be. The lack of digits also earned him his nickname, "Three-Finger Brown." Brown helped the Cubs to win the World Series in 1907 and again in 1908, both against the Detroit Tigers. Tommy Lucchese lost his right index finger in a machine shop accident when he was nineteen years old. The story holds that at a police booking, the cop taking prints noticed Lucchese's impairment and said, "Hey look, it's Three-Finger Brown!" Much to Lucchese's dismay, the nickname stuck.

Carlo Gambino

"Gambino was like the hog snake, which rolls over and plays dead until trouble passes."
—ALBERT A. SEEDMAN, NYPD CHIEF OF DETECTIVES

The photograph shows a kindly, old, Italian man. There is a distant smile on his lips, an amused gleam in his eye—his hands serenely clasped together in a beneficent pose they would seem to hold even without handcuffs necessitating it. The plain-clothed cop escorting the old man towers over his diminutive frame, yet the man does not appear fearful or intimidated. Rather the opposite, he seems oddly in control of the situation. One might never guess, looking at the photo, that in 1969 the United States Department of Justice identified this man as the head of organized crime in America.

Carlo Gambino was born in Palermo, Sicily, in 1902. Growing up in the motherland of the Italian Mafia, Gambino worked under the original godfather, Don Vito Cascio Ferro. With a wealth of experience in the Italian underworld, Gambino set out, just shy of his twentieth birthday, to try his luck in the New World. Prohibition had recently been declared the law in the United States, and word was that there were fortunes to be made delivering illicit booze to thirsty Americans. Gambino arrived in 1921, and settled in Brooklyn, New York, working for mobster Al Mineo, who at the time was loyal to mob kingpin Giuseppe

"Joe the Boss" Masseria. By the mid-1920s, Masseria was in charge of most of the criminal operations in New York. Gambino was a quiet soldier in the crime family. He did what he was told, but always kept a shrewd eye out for opportunities.

By 1930, the Castellammarese War was in full swing, with forces loyal to Joe the Boss battling those of Salvatore Maranzano for control of the underworld. Either through providence or necessity, Carlo Gambino switched sides to Maranzano. (There is some dispute as to when he

Facing Page: Carlo Gambino mug shot, c. 1930s.

Left: Gambino in FBI custody in 1970. He was arrested in connection with a plot to rob an armored car of $6 million.

Right: 1933 New York Police Department mug shot of Vincent Mangano. Albert Anastasia is believed to have had Mangano murdered to inherit the crime family. Gambino, in turn, is believed to have had Anastasia murdered.

switched sides, either before or after Masseria's murder at the hands of Charles "Lucky" Luciano and Meyer Lansky.) But Maranzano didn't have long to celebrate his victory over Masseria. His own murder would take place a scant five months later, again at the hands of Luciano and Lansky, who immediately set about organizing a nationwide crime syndicate.

Al Mineo was one of the casualties of the Castellammarese War, so in 1931 Gambino found himself under the leadership of Vincent Mangano. He formed a relationship with

---

VITAL SIGNS

Born: August 24, 1902
Died: October 15, 1976
Cause of Death: Natural causes (heart attack)
Buried: St. Johns Cemetery; Queens, New York

SCREEN TIME

Gotti (1996) (TV). Played by Marc Lawrence (with Armand Assante as John Gotti)
Between Love & Honor (1995) (TV). Played by Robert Loggia

Mangano's underboss, the murderous Albert Anastasia. The relationship between the men is hard to understand, as some reports tell of Anastasia verbally abusing and humiliating Gambino in public. But whatever acrimony Anastasia may have showed toward Gambino, he nonetheless made him his underboss when he took over the crime family reportedly by assassinating Mangano.

Other mobsters were often mystified by Anastasia's choice for number two. Gambino was seen by many as a hapless lackey. But this image was one that was carefully cultivated by Gambino. It caused his friends as well as his enemies to constantly underestimate him, dismissing him as harmless. Anastasia himself most likely bought into this image. He may have thought that by appointing a lap dog to be his underboss, that he was both protecting himself from mutiny and raising his own stature when seen in comparison with those around him. Albert Anastasia thought wrong.

In the 1950s, Vito Genovese was on the rise in the Syndicate, attempting to make his bid to be *capo di tutti capi* of American organized crime. Anastasia was a dangerous loose cannon, and his murderous ways were threatening the health and safety of the mob as a whole. Genovese contacted Gambino and assured him that he would support Gambino's promotion to boss when and if Anastasia was knocked off. Don Vito may have felt that with Gambino as head of one of New York's crime families, he could bully Gambino to do his bidding and thus widen his powerbase. Genovese, too, thought wrong.

In 1957, Anastasia met his end in a barber chair in a Manhattan hotel, and Gambino rose to take his seat on the Syndicate's Commission. With Anastasia dead, Luciano exiled to Italy, Frank Costello's forced retirement after an assassination attempt (orchestrated by Genovese), Lansky busy in Cuban gambling, and a seeming patsy in the person of Carlo Gambino installed for support, Genovese saw the time as ripe to take over the mob. But Vito overreached and his empire came crashing down when Gambino, Luciano, Lansky, and Costello conspired to set up Genovese for a fall. An elaborately constructed narcotics deal was tipped off to the Feds and landed Don Vito

in prison on a fifteen-year sentence that ended up being life when he died in 1969, still behind bars.

Genovese's death promoted Carlo Gambino to the *de facto* head of the Mafia. Gambino ran his crime family well, with a combination of quiet muscle and deft politics. Throughout his life and career in the mob, Gambino maintained an air of harmlessness that concealed a cunning and pragmatic businessman. Despite more than twenty arrests spanning over fifty years on a range of charges including tax evasion, extortion, bootlegging, and immigration charges, Gambino spent less than ten months in total behind bars, even though he had never even become a legal American citizen.

Upon his death of a heart attack in 1976, Gambino's funeral was an event, attended by hundreds of mourners, union heads, reporters, and fellow mobsters. The funeral marked the passing of one of the few and possibly the last man who could be called *capo di tutti capi* of the American Mafia.

USA 33a - 475
(EXD. 5-77)

GOVERNMENT
EXHIBIT

Left: 1976 photo of Frank Sinatra entertaining friends backstage. (Right to left): Gregory De Palma, Sinatra, Thomas Marson, Carlo Gambino, Jimmy "The Weasel" Fratianno, and in front, Richard "Nerves" Fusco. The photo was used as a evidence in a case against Fusco and De Palma. An unknown person has been blocked out at the bottom left.

Joe Bonanno

"The way of life I and my friends had chosen was but a means to attain social advancement and respectability. We didn't consider ourselves criminals."
—From *A Man of Honor,* by Joe Bonanno

After the Castellammarese War came to an end in 1931, the Syndicate was established that included five New York crime families. Those five families were each headed respectively by Charles "Lucky" Luciano, Vincent Mangano, Joseph Profaci, Tom Gagliano, and Joseph Bonanno. Thirty-two years later, in 1963, mob informer Joe Valachi testified before a Senate subcommittee on organized crime and gave name, once again, to those five New York crime families. Only one of the original family heads was still in charge, Joseph Bonanno.

Giuseppe Bonanno was born in 1905 in Castellammare del Golfo, in Palermo, Sicily, the motherland of the Italian Mafia. The son of a successful man said to have strong connections in that mafia, young Joseph and his family moved to America when he was only three years old, apparently in avoidance of legal troubles back in Italy. A challenge to family interests urged the Bonannos back to Sicily in 1912 where Joseph spent his formative years, weaned on the traditions of the Sicilian Mafia. Those traditions were built around strong codes of honor and dictated how lives were lived and business was conducted. But, as with any doctrine,

the actual practice of those codes was open to interpretation.

At fourteen, Joseph Bonanno found himself an orphan with the deaths of his parents. After attending naval school in Palermo, he set out on a journey that returned him to America. Settling in the city of his childhood, Joseph began working with a group of Castellammarese mobsters in Brooklyn. The arrival in the late 1920s of a powerful Italian Mafioso, Salvatore Maranzano, set the stage for the Castellammarese War between him and "Joe the Boss" Masseria. Bonanno naturally sided with Maranzano, as a fellow Castellammarese "man or honor." By some accounts he served as underboss to Maranzano. Ultimately, however, the war was decided by a third party, Lucky Luciano, who had both Masseria and Maranzano killed.

In the establishment of the nationwide crime Syndicate that followed, Joe Bonanno was awarded most of Maranzano's rackets and was asked to step in and serve as boss of the crime family and held a seat on the Commission.

Joe Bonanno's rackets were many and varied. He had interests in numerous legitimate businesses, including clothing manufacturing and

Opposite: Joseph "Joe Bananas" Bonanno in New York City, 1966.

a Wisconsin cheese factory. His underworld rackets included prostitution, gambling, extortion, and loansharking. One of Bonanno's businesses seemed to bridge the gap quite neatly between his legitimate and illegitimate enterprises. Apparently Bonanno owned a funeral parlor that often used two-tiered coffins to dispose of bodies no one wanted found. With the legitimate deceased on top for all to see, and a mob hit victim concealed below, the coffins appeared normal and were properly buried with no one the wiser. With his many successful business enterprises, Bonanno also began expanding his reach into different states, including Arizona and California. Bonanno was slowly accumulating enormous power and influence.

When Bonanno's closest Syndicate ally and friend, boss Joe Profaci, died in 1962, the stage was set again for another big shakeup in the mob hierarchy. There are differing versions of events that occurred after Profaci's death. The widely believed version holds that Joe Profaci was the one holding back Bonanno's ambition to dominate the Syndicate. After Profaci's death, Bonanno convinced the family's new boss, Joe Magliacco, that the time was ripe to take over. To do so, a plan was instituted to kill off many of the mob's top bosses, including Tommy Lucchese and Carlo Gambino, as well as several bosses around the country. The other version of the events derives from the Bonanno camp, which contends that the whole plot was Magliacco's idea and the Bonanno family had no knowledge or involvement in it. Whoever's plan it was, in 1963 the wheels of the massive assassination attempt were set in motion.

It was Joe Magliacco who chose the hitman for the big job, Joseph Colombo, a soldier in his own family. But Colombo did not carry out the hit as ordered. Instead, he seized on the opportunity to double cross his own boss and revealed the plot to Gambino. The Commission, upon learning of the plot, ordered both Magliacco and Bonanno to appear before them for discipline. Magliacco did as he was instructed and was ordered to pay a $50,000 fine and persuaded to retire. This relative slap on the wrist in terms of mob punishment was perhaps meant to entice Bonanno into appearing. But Bonanno refused to show. It was the beginning of the end for Bonanno's reign.

Bonanno went on the lam and attempted to set up citizenship in Canada, but was refused because he did not disclose his prior criminal involvements. Meanwhile, the Commission appointed former Bonanno family member, Gaspar DiGregorio, as boss of the family. This caused a split in the family as its members chose sides. Eventually, in October of 1964, Bonanno returned to New York and was promptly kidnapped by Buffalo crime boss (and Bonanno cousin)

─── **VITAL SIGNS** ───

Born: January 18, 1905
Died: May 11, 2002
Cause of Death: Natural causes
(heart failure)
Buried: Holy Hope Cemetery &
Mausoleum; Tucson, Arizona

─── **SCREEN TIME** ───

Bonanno: A Godfather's Story (1999)
(TV). Played by Martin Landau
*Love, Honor & Obey: The Last
Mafia Marriage* (1993) (TV).
Played by Ben Gazzara

Stefano Magaddino. The general belief is that the kidnapping was on the orders of the Commission, who did not want to just outright kill Bonanno. He still had command of a sizable number of loyal forces and could easily unleash a bloody gang war. At the time, the Syndicate was still reeling from the sensational testimony of informer Joe Valachi, and the country, still mourning the assassination of President John F. Kennedy the year before, was in no mood to tolerate a mob war.

Bonanno was held for nineteen months, during which his loyal forces under his son, Bill, fought against the forces of DiGregorio for control of the family. The conflict would become known as the "Banana War." Meanwhile negotiations between the Commission and Bonanno continued. After a deal was finally reached where Bonanno would retire but maintain his interest in western states, he was released, only to renege on the deal and launch a violent campaign to reclaim his family. His quest came to an end in 1968 when Bonanno had a heart attack and decided to call it quits. He retired to his home in Tucson, Arizona.

Joe Bonanno was brought back into the public eye when, in 1985, a crusading U.S. attorney named Rudolph W. Giuliani used Bonanno's memoirs, *A Man of Honor*, as proof that a national crime commission did exist. The resulting trial led to a combined total of 100 years in prison sentences for many of the mob's top bosses. An eighty-year-old Bonanno was called to testify but refused. He served fourteen months for contempt of court, but was released early because it was believed that his failing health would soon bring his death. He would live another seventeen years, long enough to see Rudy Giuliani become New York City mayor, and national hero after the terrorist attacks of September 11, 2001. Son Bill Bonanno said, "We've had our differences with Mr. Giuliani. But that being said, we have to tip our hat to him for how he's performed. He's done wonders and deserves most of the accolades he's received."

Joseph Bonanno died on May 11, 2002. He was the last mob boss from the time of the Castellammarese War to die. His passing marks the end of an era in the history of the American mobster.

Left: Actor Martin Landau portrayed the infamous mobster in the 1999 television movie Bonanno: A Godfather's Story.

BIBLIOGRAPHY

BOOKS

Bonanno, Joseph. *A Man of Honor: The Autobiography of Joseph Bonanno*. New York: Simon & Schuster, 1983.

Cohen, Mickey and John Peer Nugent. *In My Own Words*. Englewood Cliffs, NJ: Prentice-Hall, 1975.

Eisenberg, Dennis, Dan, Uri and Eli Landau. *Meyer Lansky: Mogul of the Mob*. New York & London: Paddington Press, Ltd. 1979.

Giancana, Sam and Chuck. *Double Cross*. New York: Warner Books, 1992.

Gosch, Martin A., and Richard Hammer. *The Last Testament of Lucky Luciano*. Boston: Little, Brown and Company, 1975.

Hammer, Richard. *The Illustrated History of Organized Crime*. Philadelphia: Running Press, 1989.

Lacey, Robert. *Little Man: Meyer Lansky and the Gangster Life*. Boston: Little, Brown and Company, 1991.

Maas, Peter. *The Valachi Papers*. New York: G.P. Putnam's Sons, 1968.

Sifakis, Carl. *The Mafia Encyclopedia*. New York: Checkmark Books, 1999.

Turkus, Burton B., and Sid Feder. *Murder, Inc.: The Story of the Syndicate*. Cambridge, Ma.: Da Capo Press, 1992.

WEBSITES

American Mafia, The, www.onewal.com

Crime Library, The, www.crimelibrary.com

FBI Freedom of Information Act, foia.fbi.gov

Find A Grave, www.findagrave.com

Internet Movie Database, www.imdb.com

Murder Inc.com, www.murderinc.com

Las Vegas Review-Journal, www.1st100.com

INDEX

Page numbers in *italics* refer to illustrations.

ACKNOWLEDGMENTS

The publisher would like to thank the individuals and agencies below for supplying the photographs:

AP Wide World Photos: pp. 9, 14, 20, 22, 23, 24, 26, 27, 28, 33, 36, 37 (top), 43, 44 (top), 45, 46, 47, 48, 49, 51, 57, 59, 60 (top), 61, 65, 69 (bottom), 70 bottom), 72, 74, 75 (top), 79, 81 (bottom), 82, 84, 90, 92, 93 (bottom), 97, 98, 100, 101, 103, 104, 105, 107, 111, 112, 113 (top), 114, 115, 117, 118, 120, 122, 124, 125, 126, 128, 129 (bottom), 130, 132, 133, 145 (top), 146, 149, 150, 152, 153

Bettmann/CORBIS: pp. 2, 4, 8-9, 11, 12, 13, 15 (bottom), 16, 17, 18, 19, 25, 29, 30, 31, 32, 34, 35, 37 (bottom), 38, 40, 41, 42, 44 (bottom), 48-49, 50, 53, 54, 55 (top), 56, 58, 60 (bottom), 62, 63, 64, 66, 68, 69 (top), 70 (top), 71, 75 (bottom), 76, 77, 78, 80 (bottom), 83, 85, 86, 88, 89 (bottom), 94, 95, 96, 108, 109, 113 (bottom), 114, 115, 116, 129 (top), 134, 135, 136, 137, 138, 140, 141, 142, 143, 144, 145 (bottom), 147

CORBIS SYGMA: p. 81 (top)

NYC Municipal Archives: pp. 52, 55 (bottom), 67, 80 (top), 93 (top), 102, 110, 114, 148

Tim Page/CORBIS: p. 106

PEMCO - Webster & Stevens Collection; Museum of History & Industry, Seattle/CORBIS: p. 8

John Springer Collection/CORBIS: pp. 15 (top), 89 (top)

Underwood & Underwood/CORBIS: p. 10